BUNS OF STEEL

The Unstoppable Pursuit of Fitness

Andre Rose

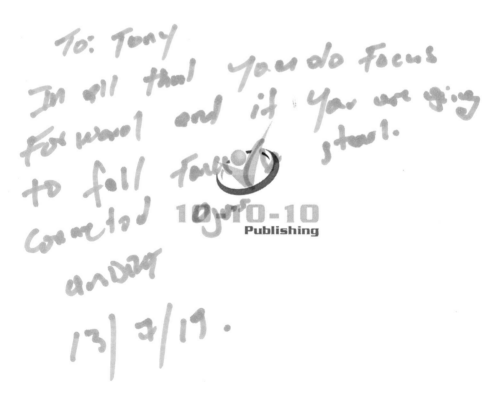

To: Tony
In all that you do Focus
Forward and if you are going
to fall Tough steel.
Corrected
andrew
13/ 7/19.

10-10
Publishing

BUNS OF STEEL
THE UNSTOPPABLE PURSUIT OF FITNESS

www.bunsofsteelbook.com

Copyright ° 2019 by Andre Rose

ISBN: 9781795808316

Publisher
10-10-10 Publishing
Markham, Ontario
CANADA

TABLE OF CONTENTS

Dedication   V
Acknowledgements and Gratitude   vii
Foreword   xi
About the Author   xiii

Chapter 1: The Most Effective Methods
of Strength Training to Suit Your Needs   1
Chapter 2: Impact on My Life   9
Chapter 3: How to Age Gracefully
With a Healthy Mind and Body   21
Chapter 4: Great Tips for Impact and Exercise   31
Chapter 5: Remedy for an Enlarged Liver, Testosterone,
Inflammation, and other Chronic Diseases   41
Chapter 6: Once a Man Twice a Child   51
Chapter 7: Men on the Assembly Line   59
Chapter 8: Effective Stretching Methods   65
Chapter 9: Understanding the Importance of Fitness   75
Chapter 10: A Life of Rewarding and Fulfilling Moments   81
Appendix "A": Mind & Hydration   93
Appendix "B": Recipes   97
Appendix "C": Exercises & Stretches   103

DEDICATION

This book is dedicated to my late grandparents, particularly my grandfather who passed away from prostate cancer. Your wisdom is what has kept me going each and every day. For as long as I can remember, the many things that you have taught me are now helping me as a grown man. There were many times you both would pull me aside to show me love and remind me that I can do great things, because it's not where you came from but where you are going that makes the difference. You have instilled so many values, which I could never have gotten in the classroom. You were a true example of the values you taught. As much as it was hard, it kept me focused. Oftentimes, I would have to reach to find it.

I miss playing in your hair, Grandma, and I am sorry I was not there to see you laid to rest. Although both of you are gone in body, I feel your spirit with me each and every day. There are many times I try to commemorate our times together. Grandma, I remember one of the many things you would say: "Humble calf suck the most milk." It is not the amount of money you earn that makes you a man; it is the amount you save. At nineteen years old, you said to me that I wasted my mornings and was now catching up on my evenings. Wow! Now, as an adult, I can fully understand what you were saying. I love you very much. Both of you were the rock of our family, and I could not have had better people to be my grandparents. God bless your soul...

ACKNOWLEDGEMENTS AND GRATITUDE

I wish to give thanks to our Lord and Savior, Jesus Christ. I would also like to thank my family and friends, the countless persons I spoke to over the years, and those who have had some impact on my life. Thanks to those who I had random conversations with at work and through my Facebook surveys. Although many of you wish to remain anonymous, I would like to acknowledge that you were selfless in offering your time and feedback. Thank you for giving me your time and entrusting me to create products and to share my insight over the years. Your contributions to my insight, knowledge, and awareness have helped in this book. I say thanks very much. To my family, the gift of having you all is incomparable. To those of you in Jamaica, I love each and every one of you. Yes, we are all apart, but spirit holds us together. Thank you all for your love, devotion, moral support, and loyalty. To the **Lyles** family, I can't thank you enough; you all took me in as family, and you made me feel welcome.

To my mother, **Rosalee 'Rosie' Newman,** you are my most treasured asset. Thank you for your support and for showing me what love is. Yes there were differences, many times, but you were still there when I needed someone to talk to. We may not always see eye to eye on everything, but your love has not gone unnoticed. I only wanted you to be proud of me. I can still, till this day, taste some of your amazing carrot juice and some rice and peas. You did the best you could for me and my other two sisters, and for that, I want to say thanks very much.

To my father, **Denham Rose**, thank you for having done what you could at a late stage in my life.

To my **sisters** and **brothers,** love is the greatest tool we all have. We are all over the globe working to create our own lives. Love you all very much.

To two of the most important people in my life, **Peter Martin** and **Lorna Martin,** where do I begin? The both of you have been more than a father and mother to me. I have learned so much from you both about life and the ability to achieve everything in life. Eleven years of constant teachings on the foundations of fitness, and sending us to the gym, has shaped my entire career on what I see myself doing in the fitness industry. I could not have been the man I am today if it wasn't for the teachings and sales experience from your business. Your ongoing support has empowered me to go after my dreams, and has molded me into the confident person I am today. Your life teachings on retail, business, and life skills have enabled me to start my own company, and for that, I'm very grateful.

Thanks to **Shandell** for helping me to get started on this book. As you said, when we first met, there was something you had to do for me, and you certainly came through for me.

To **Hugh Simmonds**, you are such a remarkable person. We had many conversations at Collectibles, when you would come to buy your shoes. We shared a lot, and many people wondered if we were brothers. You knew that there was a special person trying to be born, as I needed guidance. You said I was like a can of coca. When you pop me, there would be a tremendous amount of energy. And that it is. Thanks very much for taking my phone calls late at night and early in the morning. I am a better person because of those conversations. You shared your home and your wisdom to my betterment, and for that I am very grateful.

To my **co-workers** at Serta Mattress Company and Collectibles, you guys helped make this book possible. So many experiences I have gained from you over the years, and for that I'm thankful. Much love for all the support and help.

To my very good friends, **Shawn Cuffie** and **Leigh-Ann Hearn,** words can't express how thankful I am for the years of friendship. You put up with so much of my comings and goings. Leigh-Ann, you are more than a friend to me; you're more like a sister. Thank you for the tough love you gave me when it was necessary. Thank you for standing by me when my strength failed me. For the incomparable love, care, and support you gave in my trying moment, I say thank you. You loved me in spite of my faults. As you would always say, "I love you for who you are, Dre'."

I would like to extend my gratitude to the following individuals for giving me their support, patience, input, love, and time. Success is the fruits of personal effort, plus support and encouragement from people like you: **Gary Stewart,** Annie **Tuck**, **Barbara Marshall,** **Marlene**, and the **Lyles** family. To my very special friend, **Sharene Ankle**, we spent lots of late nights chatting, masterminding with each other, as we know that iron sharpens iron. I knew from the day we met, we would become friends. Thanks for hearing what I had to chat about, and for reminding me of what having a personal relationship with God is all about.

FOREWORD

Among the many profound revelations, Andre Rose will reveal to you a fundamental approach to harnessing faith and believing in your dreams. Reading this inspiring book, Buns of Steel: The Unstoppable Pursuit of Fitness, will help you break out of your mediocrity and negative mindset, and get you onto a new, exhilarating, passionate path of divine purpose and a life of freedom. I suggest you read it well and take a step toward truly living a life you love. The lessons within this book will teach you how to take care of external and internal health issues that may arise. It will guide you on how to start on your journey to fitness through dieting for your body type, exercising the right way to see results, battling chronic conditions, and meditating correctly. It will also guide you on how to overcome personal struggles, and provide a gateway to finding your own happiness.

Self-development is a vital tool for you, and it is worth learning and understanding. It is not only a practical primer, but a way of understanding the elements to finding your vision. Far too often you play victim to the circumstances you encounter throughout your life. This is where this amazing book will tell you how to overcome and create your own dream. Behind every problem you have, there's a question to be asked, and an answer to be revealed. Behind every answer there's an action to be taken, and a new way of life to be born.

By reading this book you will gain full insight into the hurdles Andre had to face in life, so that you can gain strength and wisdom to move forward in your life, with both remarkable and commendable results.

Raymond Aaron
New York Times Bestselling author

ABOUT THE AUTHOR

I was born in Manchester, Jamaica. I'm the second of three children for my mother, and the third of seven for my father. I lived with my grandmother and other family members for a long period of my early childhood (as my mother worked in the capital city, Kingston, to make ends meet and provide for all of us, as best as she could). My mother worked as a housekeeper, and a very good one too. I can remember, many times, she would come home to visit in Manchester, at my grandmother and grandfather's house. She would clean and do house chores. As a boy, she told me that I would always want her to kiss me on the lips, in order to leave some of her lipstick on me. I was from a very large family; our family home was very busy. My grandmother was a strict disciplinarian who believed in doing the right things at all times. She was also very involved in the church. Wednesdays were for prayer meeting, Thursdays were for choir practice, and Sundays were for Sunday Service.

At the age of nine, I was sent to live with my grand uncle. I had no choice but to go and live with him; as a child, I had to do what I was told. He had just lost his wife and, therefore, needed some support. His house was a two-bedroom house. All of my grand uncle's family members were all living in the capital city, Kingston, so they asked my grandmother if I could live with him for some time, and she said yes. In my grand uncle's house, there were lots of fruit trees. I was very happy to go and live with him because there were all kinds of fruits and endless amounts to eat. The yard had all kinds of fruits but also an abundant supply of vegetables. I also enjoyed climbing the grapefruit, orange, and mango trees. I had full access to them all. My grandmother would buy fruits and vegetables: pineapples, yams, bananas, apples, oranges, and many other delights, from my grand uncle to take to the market and sell.

My father lived in Toronto, Canada. I met him when I was fourteen years old. I didn't see much of my dad during this period. Though I met him at fourteen, he was never around very much, at least not as often as I would hope, especially for a young man like myself. Quite frankly, whenever he visited Jamaica, I saw him as a stranger, and I really wasn't fond of him. He lived in Canada, and I had no contact with him. To this day, our level of communication is quite limited.

I love nature, and I'm very passionate about life. For that reason, I had a desire to seek out a greater understanding of nature and life through higher education. I went to Winston Jones High School, Knox Community College, and Northern Caribbean University, all in Jamaica.

While attending Knox Community College, with the sewing experience I got while living with my grandmother, I was able to secure employment at Clove and P. S. as a seamstress. After leaving the parish of Manchester, I moved to Kingston, where I also worked as a seamstress at a local dressmaking shop, in the same house in which I was living. While working for that local dressmaking shop, I happened to visit a business office in town, where I met the owner of a company called Collectibles, one of Jamaica's largest department stores in the capital, Kingston. In no time, I was working for Collectibles, and I spent eleven years there before I moved to Toronto, Canada.

One of the most amazing things about me is that I love to win friends and influence others. I was a professional retail sales specialist, and personal shopper, for Collectibles in Kingston, and now I am the fashion designer for STEELE by Andre Rose.

I'm a result oriented and highly motivated professional with a background in wardrobe styling, retail sales management, and customer satisfaction. I have an extraordinary ability to maintain long-term relationships through quality customer service and excellent organizational and communication skills, and I also possess the ability to multitask. Needless to say, I am ambitious and resourceful, with a can-do attitude that thrives in an entrepreneurial and fast paced environment. I am proud to be a Jamaican native who loves to travel, shop, attend church and art exhibitions, and meet new diverse and colourful individuals. All things fitness, fashion, art, and beauty-related attracts my interest and gets my attention. I am motivated by my ability to break down barriers and inspire others through style and faith. My clients grow to trust me with their fashion statement. I am very responsible, and I easily see what is illogical because I am passionate about everything I do. I will continue to grow and inspire others through my love of fashion.

You have a chance to get bonus/additional materials. Simply go to www.bunsofsteelbook.com, and enter for a chance to win a weekend stay at Friday Harbour resort on Lake Simcoe.

From Toronto, Friday Harbour is so much closer than cottage country; although it feels like a world away, this close escape is only 45 minutes from the G.T.A., and is accessible by Go train.

Chapter 1

The Most Effective Methods of Strength Training to Suit Your Needs

The most effective way of strength training is using your own body weight or low intense weight repetition for maximum result. Training splits are also great for intermediate to advance gym goers. For beginners, I recommend starting a full body workout, 3–4 days a week, for 1–1.5 hours. Tempo is important because it is the rate in which the eccentric speed works with the concentric. Using, for example, 0:3:1:0 tempo allows for safer exercise, as well as better mind- body connection to the muscle and brain, which is better for muscle growth. Learning by observing is one of the best ways of learning. What you need to do in making your exercises effective is to train with someone who has more experience, or ask questions from other individuals who show an interest in what you do. There are people that take a great interest in helping others, and there are other strategic ways of learning how to train your body on a basic level of fitness.

At the start of my years, I attended bodybuilding competitions so that I could get more knowledge on my body and fitness as a whole, to better understand the fitness lifestyle. I fell in love with fitness, and little did I know that one day I would be on stages competing with other lovers of fitness. Standing aside and watching can be invaluable; learning from others will help you better understand your body for any abnormal development. Once you have a clear idea of what works and what doesn't, you can begin to create an action plan for your own achievements. I have used this in my own approach at the beginning of my journey in this amazing lifestyle. At first, there will be a slow start to this lifestyle, but endurance and frequency are the two most important things you will need to substantiate your progress.

Endurance is knowing that it's not going to come overnight, but that it is an ongoing process and will therefore lead to longer lasting frequency. The process will not be easy, but if you keep the finish goal in mind, it will inspire you along the way. Endurance is the key factor to maintain a lasting tolerance. Over the years, there have been many individuals that have begun a lifestyle in fitness, but then, somehow, fell out of love with the process, not realizing that they are giving up on the benefits of exercise. The best strength training that's universal for any body type is using your own body weight to exercise at a minimal pace. What is a good weight? A good weight is 185 lbs.-195 lbs. for a man. The right weight for an individual depends on a number of factors, which include structure, genes, and background. An athlete who is a competitive bodybuilder competes at a different weight class. Those athletes may have been heavier in weight but will then have to reduce their weight so that they can fit in their appropriate weight class.

For recreational athletes, a man's body weight should be between 10-20 percent fat, and a woman's should be between 15 and 25 percent fat. A body fat percentage is a good guideline, even if you're not a recreational athlete. The American population is a great example of individuals who carry more fat than their required body weight. The reason is because everything is readily accessible, so they do not take into consideration what they are putting in their bodies. I have noticed that most tend to overeat past their set limit and, therefore, they cannot differentiate when they are satisfied and when they are full. Being satisfied is eating within a measured amount without feeling uncomfortable when you eat. Being full is not eating within the measured amount for your body, and therefore you feel uneasy. In fact, as I've been saying, the pursuit of fitness is you having a level of understanding that any form of exercise will prolong your ability to live longer. Fitness has become a life saver for many individuals who face daily challenges with heart disease, bone disease, and mental stress.

Let's look at body fat for the average population. There are many people who have more than 30 percent body fat. In fact, 40 percent are considered obese. If you have more than 30 percent body fat, you are distinctly overweight, and this is unhealthy. It's going to affect how long you live, and it's going to cut down your quality of life every single day. It also impacts our government's ability to provide greater health care for its citizens. In order to help to bring more awareness to obesity, we must educate people about the importance of fitness and living a healthier life.

I would advise a man who has 20 percent of body fat, and a woman who has 25 to 35 percent body fat, to start thinking about increasing exercise and decreasing their intake of calories. Once you drop below 10 percent body fat, you're underfed, which means that you are not getting enough nutrition. This affects a very small percentage of the population, but the majority of us are over fed. If there is a system that can inform you how to measure and use techniques on how much water is in your body, or how much bone mass, and how much muscle, a well-trained qualified professional can help you determine the ratio of body fat in your overall weight, through different methods. Knowing how much body fat you carry is the starting point from which to begin to make healthy decisions. Do something about your excess fat, even if you don't take fat measurement tests. If you look at your naked body in the mirror, and there's 2 or 3 inches of fat hanging over your waist, it's likely that you have too much body fat.

Overcoming Body Weight

Battling in the fat wars and being overweight is not a comfortable or healthy way to live. It is too much for a particular body type. People dramatically shorten the length of their lives and severely compromise energy and the sense of wellbeing. Why do we get overweight quite simply by not doing enough physical activity and eating too much? In past generations, to survive, work teams had a lot of physical work to get through in a day, but as our society develops, labor saving devices, such as tractors and washing machines in the workplace, have become more sedentary; therefore, we cease the benefits of the physical demands of activity. Also, we have to take into account that the average age in our society is getting older. As we get older, we tend to be less active and have a tendency to put on more weight. Another factor is that we eat the wrong foods, in huge proportions. We're in the age of having to supersize everything, and it is killing us. The emphasis should not be to get full but rather to get full enjoyment and nutritious benefit. Does this food fuel my body properly and enjoyably? We tend to love French fries, gravy, and ice cream, but these are the foods we have to stay away from, because we're not living the active life of our cave dwelling ancestors. What you have to do, in terms of what you eat, is take a good look at each meal and ask how it serves your health. It's not a matter of making you feel guilty, but in the same token, the spun of guilt is involved every time we eat too much. Don't beat yourself up if you fall off the calorie wagon from time to time. Just get back on, to continuous sensible eating. Crash diets are not the answer either. It's very important to get the nutritional balance. The only sure way to lose weight and to have a good life is to eat sensibly and do regular physical activity. Change supersize into exercise.

Factoring in eating and exercise plays a crucial role in weight control, but eating patterns must also be factored in. It's possible to be fit and fat; you can exercise a lot and still weigh a lot. It is not about how much you eat but is about the quality of food that contains any protein complex, carbohydrates, fruits, or vegetables, which makes more sense than just fat, such as greasy French fries. First, when mastering exercising, you'll most likely put on weight. The first month or 2, you will gain 3 to 4 pounds of muscle. Muscle weighs more than fat but takes up less area. A full week of muscle training will eventually translate into an overall reduction of body fat. If you lose the body fat and replace it with muscle, your weight will gradually be where it's supposed to be, and you will feel much healthier and stronger. Trust the process and be patient, because it works. I never encourage people to modify the process by not eating, or by restricting their diets. Process strength training, and take enough vitamins, as well as nutritious supplements, to keep you on a constant and improving process.

Everyone can lose weight, but it's easier said than done. Yes, it does require a lot of time and devotion, but you cannot get to your weight goal if you're stuck in old patterns. Getting the weight off can become a major challenge; however, there is a relatively easy way to do it. It may take some time, but you can do it. In order to lose weight, you have to eat within the calories for your body, age, and lifestyle. You have to exercise to burn more calories than the Mountains take. In order for it to be effective, you need to lose 4 pounds a month, and that is a reasonable goal. Slow and steady wins the race. Slow weight loss is permanent weight loss. Fast weight loss means that it may come back quicker, so when you examine the food you eat, you can change the way you eat some foods. For example, you could buy bread that tastes good without needing butter.

There are many whole grain breads with different types of seeds, such a sunflower seeds, and they taste delicious just by themselves. If you need to put something on the bread for more substance, you can add small amounts of butter, olive oil, palm oil, flax seeds, or avocado puree. Eat good fats as opposed to bad fats. And don't slather; putting on just a thin layer of butter is best. Consider how many calories are needed in a portion to eat. There's nothing wrong with calories that fuel your body, but there's a lot wrong with calories that just control the energy of the body. Exercise is the number one way to lose weight, and strength training builds up your muscles. Strength training has the added advantage of burning calories for up to 48 hours after exercising, in the process of continuing to build muscle. If you want a healthy weight, do 2 things: eat less, and carefully pick what you eat. Exercise, and do strength training to build stronger muscles, and you will burn fat very quickly. Ninety percent of your exercise is what you do at home. You spend less time in the gym than at home, so it is important to make sure that you maintain a healthy lifestyle at home.

This chapter teaches you how to strength train your body, overcome body weight, and to understand and know your body—knowing that any physical activity you do counts, as well as choosing better choices when related to food. In the next chapter, you will learn about my fitness journey and diet remedies on how to control body fat.

Notes

Chapter 2

Impact on My Life

In 2002, when my boss decided that he was going to send his employees to the gym, I did not fully understand what he was doing. Now that I am a grown man, about to turn 39 years, I have come to understand what fitness can do to one's life. At first, when I started, I had no understanding of what I was doing; but somehow it seemed like it was going to be rather nice and easy to stick with. At first, there were about 14-15 of us when my boss decided to send us to the gym. I found it interesting how we huddled in a little ford hatchback van. We would go to the gym on Tuesdays and Thursdays. Somehow, to me, it felt nice when I walked into the facility and saw the weight machines. We had an instructor who taught us to use the weights, but I was so excited that I didn't even wait for the trainer to give me instructions. I started to exercise by observing what other people in the gym were doing. We would work out for an hour and a half, and then we would all get back in the van. It was close to another well-known gym in Jamaica, called Spartan Health Club. After we all hopped in the van, going back home, I couldn't wait for tomorrow to come, because going to the gym seemed rather interesting.

This method of transporting went on for a couple of weeks. Soon after, some of the employees decided that they were going to stop coming, but I was persistent on going to the gym. The group of fifteen reduced to only four, and the four of us seemed to be very faithful. We continued going to the gym for a very long time. That lasted for about two and half years. I was so excited. Over the two and half years, I started to see improvement in my body, and I was more than pleased. Soon after, it reduced to three people.

Unfortunately, in 2004, there was a hurricane, which really damaged the island. Fitness was put on hold for a while; we had no electricity, as most places didn't have any. The stores were boarded up, so we could not go to work, but after a few days, we went back to work, and many other places had electricity. Because there were damages, for the first couple of days, we left work early; so, in this case, we were never able to go to the gym. I was really heartbroken. I was more heartbroken when my boss decided that he was no longer going to pay for us to go to the gym. I was shocked. So, for about a year, I was not able to go to the gym. I had also moved from home as well, so there was a little bit of distance from where the gym was to my home.

On my way home, there was another gym, called Uptown Fitness, on Constant Spring Road. It was in an upstairs building, so the name of the gym and the price could easily be seen. I could see the price of the membership but could not afford it. I would often think to myself that one day I would go to that gym. One day, I decided to go check out the facility. I felt timid because this gym was much bigger than the one I used to go to, and there were much more muscular men. I walked around the gym, and I saw exercise equipment I had not seen before. At this time, I decided that I was going to sacrifice and get a membership. Even though this was much closer to home, I would still have to take two buses to return home in the evenings. Not long after, a long- time friend, who lived in the same city, contacted me. I found out that he lived and worked in the same area that I did, and was attending the same gym, so he could give me rides in the evenings, and this made it easier for me to go home. Even though he lived and worked in the same area, he would not always want to go to the gym. I would still go because I was very determined.

Now I can understand why my boss was so successful: he was determined. It is because of him that I am so determined today. I owe a lot to him and his wife for the endless amount of support they showed me while I worked with them. I would admire my boss because he was very smart and successful. At first, when I met him, I was very shy to speak with him, but he saw something special in me. Whenever he came to the store, he would look to find his top sales people. I also understand why he would send us to the gym so that we could do lots of sales. When he would come to the store, he would look for us to find out what the customers were saying. It was the feedback from the customers that influenced his buying power. After saving up enough money, I realized that I would be able to pay for my gym membership, and that continued for many years. After paying for my membership, I started to work out again. I started to realize my body was changing again. My arms were getting bigger, and other individuals started to take notice. I continued to train, because there was a greater love that developed.

According to the fitness and wellness professional, coach, and certified canfitpro, Gregory Dawson, during his first year in high school, his friends did not see him for 2 months because he started working out at home. He shed a lot of fat and obtained large amounts of muscle; he literally became the big dog at his high school. Fitness has allowed him to meet different people from all walks of life. It has given him the opportunity to touch the lives of those around him. He has become a sponsored athlete, has travelled, and continues to travel to different countries. One struggle he had was getting people to understand that fitness isn't just a weekend mission; it's a lifestyle change. He advises people to be patient and to understand that getting to the best health takes time. For example, it takes 25 years to get to 400 lbs., and the weight is not going to come off overnight.

Fitness and Wellness Professional, Coach and Certified Canfitpro,
Gregory Dawson

Dieting for Your Body Type

There is a difference between dieting and controlling the way you eat. Dieting is the reduction of the proportion of food we eat, because we tend to take in more without considering our body type, lifestyle, or activity level. This is different from just cutting back from eating. Controlling your eating means taking the calories needed to balance nutrition from different food groups. It means making wise choices; for example, choosing a baked potato over French fries, or oil and vinegar dressing on a salad over creamy ranch dressing. When you control your eating patterns within the proper number of calories for your lifestyle, and incorporate any strength training, you're going to get a much more effective result. If you could strength train up to 80 percent of what you invest in your exercises, your muscles will develop much quicker. If you strength train almost every day, you will burn off fat, and the food you consume will be used to build muscle. The key to a good weight is to be within your normal range, as well as incorporating exercises into your routine.

One of the misconceptions about actual size and weight control is that you need to do a lot of cardiovascular training to burn calories. You need cardiovascular exercise to improve your heart, lungs, and your whole system. To me, achieving a good weight is not about denying yourself food; it's about a balance. In fact, when we control our eating habits, it shouldn't be painful; it should include enough leeway to allow occasional indulgences in your diet. You can design your weight control program to allow you to have a few perks. Many people seek a professional weight control program from companies that claim to guarantee a certain level of weight loss. Within a certain length of time, any control program or group that does not encourage exercise is not telling the whole story. Control programs that encourage exercise, along with a balanced diet that doesn't encourage extremes, is okay. I think the best of these programs are those that teach us to make healthy choices so we can continue on our own. We owe it to ourselves to make sure that we stay true to a healthy lifestyle. When you add protein to your diet, it increases your muscle size. Dieting and following a specific regime is not easy. In order to have an effective diet regime, one has to be consistent to make sure that they achieve the results they want.

This is a regime that my friend, Shawn Cuffie, follows, and it works best for him because he is consistent with it. In his diet, he eats whatever he wants, but he makes sure that they are smaller portions. He does not eat to get full, but he makes sure that he is satisfied. His workout regime is a great tip to follow if you do not enjoy being at the gym. Making sure you are implementing exercise every day is very vital in the process. He has added apple cider vinegar, which works well to help maintain his diet progression. It is all about finding what works best for your body while staying nourished and achieving your weight loss goal.

Drink

- Water (When I'm hungry, I will have a glass of water, then a small meal.)
- Lemon Water (1 or 2 glasses first thing in the morning)
- Apple Cider Vinegar (ACV), (1 glass of water with 3 spoons of ACV before bed)
- Green drink day – kale, apple, cucumber, carrot (2 days per week, I only drink a green liquid mix.)
- Real homemade fruit drink, 3x per week (banana, strawberry, almond milk, honey, and ice)
- I consume a total of 6-8 glasses of water a day.

Note: This helps keep me full and hydrated.

Eat

- Low carbs, always
- I only use honey to sweeten drinks or in food.
- No more than 1 spoon of brown rice, maybe 3x max per week)
- A half plate of salad with lunch and dinner
- A small portion of mostly chicken breast but other meats as well
- No more than 4 slices of bread per week
- I practice intermittent fasting; therefore, eating only between 11am-6pm.

Note: I eat what I want in small portions, 4-5 times a day. I don't eat to get full but to feel satisfied.

Work out at home

- Short workouts, 4-5 days a week. I work out for 30-45 minutes, including 10 minutes of cardio with each workout, which includes running on the spot, jumping jacks, push-ups, 6 minutes of abs, glutes, squats, climbing the stairs, and other

bodyweight exercises and stretches.
- This is done first thing in the morning to be sure I complete it and get it out of the way.

Note: I work out because it makes me feel fresh throughout the day; it keeps my body feeling loose, and I feel clear of mind. It noticeably releases stress and puts me in a greater mood.

Mind

- I think slim.
- I self-talk, and this helps me believe I am trimming up.
- I look at positive body images every day, which motivates me to work for what I want.
- I tell myself the truth: I know this will take about 3 weeks before I start feeling and noticing a difference.
- I keep my eye on the prize, realizing my weight loss goal.

When you succeed in losing 10 percent of your body weight, it calls for celebration, because losing weight is an overall, long process. The resolution to keep it off for a year is possible. Make sure to implement fasting to your daily routine, at least twice a week, to allow the body to eat away any built up bacteria. Fasting is common amongst many African American cultures. I can remember, as a young boy, going to church with my aunt on a Thursday, and we would have to abstain from eating the night before so that we could start our fasting in the morning. Fasting, as a way of losing weight, has become mainstream, and is commonly called intermittent fasting. Intermittent fasting means abstaining from food for as long as you can. Try to do things that will keep you occupied and make you less hungry, so that you do not feel tired quickly. Allow your mind to do the work for you. Stay positive, and understand that intermittent fasting will help you lose weight but will also help you to flush the bacteria the body stores.

Measuring the waist to hip ratio will help you lose body fat, and will increase your vigor and overall health. Too much fat on your abdomen, stomach, and thighs puts stress on your overall body. Sometimes it causes you to have shortness of breath, and your internal organs may be more at risk of diabetes, cardiovascular disease, and some cancers. In order to understand your body, you need to constantly be observant. Take time out of your busy day to be at ease with yourself, and you should be able to tell the difference in your body. A simple way to tell if you're making progress is to measure your waist and observe the changes as you implement your exercise routine over time. This is far more effective than just weighing yourself on a scale. Remember to not strive for perfection but to make your goal to strive for a better version of yourself. The difference in the way you feel will be expressed through your body, mind, and soul. This will keep you motivated to keep going at a gradual pace until you reach the weight that is just right for you.

Most doctors would tell injured individuals not to exercise. It's well known that physical activity after injury can help speed up the healing process, and that's the reason why medical professionals get you out walking within 24 hours of having surgery. Yes, you will certainly need to modify your exercise routine after an injury, but you should not have to stop exercising. When two people always go to the gym to work out, and suddenly one falls off, the concept of entitlement robs you of your freedom; you're limiting yourself of your fitness goal, at the expense of being used to always having a workout partner. Well, you have to realize that happiness is a personal choice about taking control of your own life, and that your fitness is within the limits of your fitness goals. You can injure yourself from overtraining, which can happen to anyone, but remember to never stop exercising.

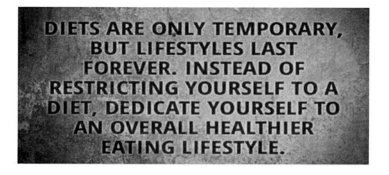

DIETS ARE ONLY TEMPORARY, BUT LIFESTYLES LAST FOREVER. INSTEAD OF RESTRICTING YOURSELF TO A DIET, DEDICATE YOURSELF TO AN OVERALL HEALTHIER EATING LIFESTYLE.

My fitness journey was never easy, but I knew what I wanted to achieve, and I made sure I followed through on what I wanted. I believe this chapter will guide you to put what you want to achieve at the forefront, when it comes to fitness. It will navigate you to a better and healthier lifestyle. Aging gracefully takes work, and you have to consistently work at it. It involves meditation, sleeping well, and mindset building, and that is what the next chapter will teach you.

Notes

Impact on My Life

Notes

Chapter 3

How to Age Gracefully
With a Healthy Mind and Body

All throughout my time exercising, I would take supplements to maintain strength and to gain body mass. Somehow, that just seems to never work for me at all, but I would try to eat as much as I possibly could. I would stock up on weight gainers and pre-workout drinks. I would oftentimes go to the doctor to get my regular check-up, and I was very interested to know my body. I was taking care of my body. One of the things I learned, as I became older, was to meditate. Meditation has helped me to find balance and a clear mind. Bob Proctor, from the Proctor Gallagher Institute, says that *"silence is the jewel of wisdom."* I think this was in reference to silencing the mind, which helps you to reduce stress, prolong life, and slow aging.

If any symptoms pertain to you right now, the chances are that you are overstressed. See it as your time. Understand what it takes to relax. Many of us do not really know how to do this. Focus on what is important, and that is you. Your exercise is important because it helps to prolong your life by many years. With everything that is happening around us, we just can't seem to shut our minds down; we hardly have time to allow our minds to take a break in order to have better clarity in our thoughts. In all situations, we should practice deep breathing techniques. Deep breathing techniques are incredibly helpful. Try simple breathing exercises, such as slowly inhaling while counting to 5 in your head; hold your breath for 5 seconds then exhale slowly. Repeat this 10 times, whenever you feel your stress levels are going up. The breathing exercises may get you into a meditative state.

There are many meditative practices that are simple and easy to incorporate into your daily life. Just before bed, I would go backwards from when I woke up in the morning, and reflect on everything that happened throughout the day; and I would do this just before I fall asleep. Allowing the mind to be free from everything that happened throughout the day, with easy breathing techniques, helps to clear the mind from unwanted happenings that took place throughout the day. Try these techniques in small increments, and gradually increase as time goes by. Your mind is like a computer processor, and you absorb everything that happens throughout the day because of the abundance of information around you.

When you allow the mind to relax before going to bed, you are allowing your conscious mind to take hold of your thoughts, so that it is in control. This helps in aging because you are less stressed. It's like getting your car serviced; if you do not take care of your car, it will eventually break down. It applies in the same way as taking care of ourselves, and meditation helps restore our minds. Sit on a comfortable chair, with your feet on the floor, and allow your breathing to flow easily while focusing on positive thoughts. You can enhance the environment with soft calming music, which is another anti-stress alternative.

If you're at your desk all day, take a walk down the hall and stretch. Actually, this is good advice for any time or place. You can stretch your neck muscles by trying to touch each shoulder with your hands. Slowly look right; then look up at the ceiling, gradually, while hanging your upper body down towards the floor. Then look left, and then rotate each shoulder in a circle. It should feel really good. For the whole body, it will release tension, and it will open up the chest by extending the arms towards both sides. Hold all the muscles in your body simultaneously for 5 seconds; then release. Hold your breath, if you choose, while engaging the abs. It should feel marvelous. Refuse to allow yourself to feel pressured; realize that there are some obligations you just may have to give up during your busiest time.

Don't make exercise one of the things you give up. If you can continue to do 30 minutes of exercise, 3 times a week, you will realize that your body will thank you, as well as your family and friends, because you will be so much more energetic and much less stressed out.

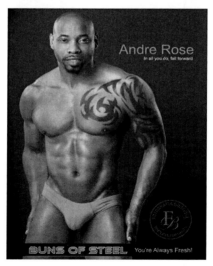

Fitness and Chronic Conditions

Let's say you have a shoulder that always hurts; it is important to engage the shoulder in moderate exercise. The two things you need to do are, first, reduce the stress in that particular shoulder, and secondly, exercise the shoulder so that the pain pressure becomes more bearable. Your body always fails at its weakest link; it is your job to make your weakest link as strong as it can be. For many of us, our weakest link takes the form of some kind of chronic condition: a threat from diabetes, chronic fatigue syndrome, heart disease, and asthma. A chronic condition is different from an injury. With an injury, you hope for recovery, and this can keep you motivated and rebuilding your exercise. The second phase is self-pity. Many times, there will be situations that will happen, but never stay down; always rise and move forward. Having self-pity is not enough reason to not do your exercises. There are many individuals that are double amputees, and they never self-pity themselves, because they accept their situation and continue on in life, doing some of the most amazing things. They serve as an inspiration to others. A chronic condition should not deter you from exercising; it should, rather, motivate you to keep going in order to be better.

The third phase is the choice between giving in or fighting. Fighting is the only thing that should motivate you in overcoming your chronic conditions. For the past year, I have been going to my doctor to learn more about my body—sometimes just from feeling slight aches and pain, but I think it's probably from the many years of exercising. Even though I may be young, I can still feel my body changing. The older you get, the more likely it is that you will have chronic conditions to deal with as you age. We need to learn how to deal with these conditions. As I get older, it has allowed me to be happier and to be more caring. It made me not take things for granted. When I was much younger, I felt that I was a better looking person. The older I get, I am realizing that the body will go through different challenges, but if you have a chronic condition, and you improve your quality of life by managing well, your sense of life values will increase. By understanding that you have only one life to live, you will start caring for yourself so that you will live a longer and more fulfilling life.

Many chronic conditions, such as diabetes, arthritis, or chronic fatigue are insidious because you can't see them, but these conditions can be turned around to be life enhancing, and that depends on how you choose to react to them. Taking control by doing something about it will give you hope. In the fitness industry, we find that we work with more people who have chronic conditions. It is the decision of making the best of what is happening in your life, or choosing to decide to make things worse. There are people who do incredible things despite great odds. If you even try to improve your health and fitness, congratulate yourself, and feel good, because many people are not even trying. If you have a chronic condition, doing fitness is not going to cure you, but you will increase your quality of life. Minimize the impact of the condition, and maximize your opportunities for health and well-being.

Depression is the most widely prevalent mental health problem, yet many times it is undiagnosed. Undiagnosed health problems can cause severe situations in families. In February, George received a phone call from Michelle. She was calling to find out if he had heard from his son. George's son was missing for 6 hours, after his girlfriend came home from work, and couldn't be found. George told Michelle he had only heard from his son in the morning. Shortly after that, George received a phone call from the police. The police claimed that George's son committed a pre-planned suicide. They deducted from his prognosis that he had a mental health condition. Vast numbers of people suffer in silence, despite advances in treatment; and many people do not realize that simple measures, like exercising, have a very beneficial effect on their moods. I'm not suggesting that people take themselves off their medication; however, there are many medications that can help you elevate your mood and fight depression, and exercising happens to be the first one that I recommend. Whenever you exercise, your body naturally produces endorphins that make you feel good, more energetic, and more productive. There's also the role of the neurotransmitter, serotonin, which has been linked to mood. Researchers found that regular exercise will alter serotonin levels, and can lead to an increased sense of well- being.

Aside from these changes in your brain chemistry, there are many other benefits from using exercise as a natural mood enhancer. First, you will experience a boost to your self-esteem by taking an active role in your own recovery. Secondly, social support contributes to a sense of connectedness, which is important for mood. Thirdly, exercise brings up stress chemicals in your body, such as adrenaline, and it helps to reduce irritability, which is often a side effect of clinical depression. Fourthly, the pleasant mood induced may help to break the cycle of pessimistic thinking, and give you a renewed sense of hope. It's possible that if you exercise regularly, you will even be able to reduce the amount of antidepressant medication, but always do this only with a doctor's advice. Become a participant in your own healthcare, and an active partner in breaking the cycle of depression so that you can live.

Mindset Building

I live in the abundance of everything around me. I'm grateful for the little things, as those little things have allowed me to appreciate big possibilities. Having a vision in mind of what you want your body to look like will enable you to achieve the physical appearance you want, if you put in the effort and the work. It's like going into the CN tower in Toronto, Canada: you cannot see the distance when you are on the first floor, but as you go up higher, you are able to see further in the distance. While you're on the first floor, you can only imagine what is to come. This helps you create a vision of what you are about to encounter. It's the same process your body goes through, because you do not have an understanding of the end result.

In 1998, the infamous movie, *How Stella Got Her Groove Back*— which was well acted by Angela Bassett, Taye Diggs, and Whoopi

Goldberg—was a movie I saw, which captivated my attention. Taye Diggs' body was the image I had in mind of how I wanted to look. Throughout the 17 years of my pursuit of fitness, I have held that image, and continually work at achieving that look. Dreams should never be evaluated according to their size; that's not what determines their worth. A dream doesn't have to be big; it just has to be bigger than you are. Shoot for the moon—even if you miss, you'll land among the stars. Only as high as I can reach, I can grow. Only as far as I can see, can I go. Only as deep as I can look, can I see. Keep your dreams alive. Understand that to achieve anything, it requires faith; and believe in yourself. Envision hard work, determination, and dedication. Remember, all things are possible for those who believe.

Having a healthy mind is rewarding. Cultivate the person who you hope to become. You are the creator of your own reality*; create that vision of who you want to become, and live that way. It all begins with the mindset approach. Transforming your way of thinking is where it starts. You ought to have positive thoughts, which will then trigger another reinforcement for you to continue to be in alignment with the person you hope to become. According to *Think and Grow Rich*, by Napoleon Hill, *"the world is filled with an abundance of opportunity, which the dreamers of the past never know. A burning desire to be and to do is the starting point from which the dreamer must take off. Dreams are not born of indifference, laziness, or lack of ambition. Remember that all who succeed in life get off to a bad start and pass through many heartbreaks and struggles before they arrive. The turning point in the lives of those who succeed usually comes at the moment of some crisis, through which they are introduced to their 'other selves.'"*

Mental detoxification helps with clearing out the mind, to help disable distractions throughout the day, and to enable positive thinking.
- Wake up gently with only invited thoughts.
- Open your mouth slightly.

- Clear the busy energy around you.
- Empty some of your thoughts by writing them down.
- Activate your senses.
- Distract your thoughts.
- Correct your breath.

Sleeping is vital to our health because it helps maintain a healthy balance of hormones that make you feel hungry. When we don't get enough sleep, it increases the risk of heart disease, kidney disease, high blood pressure, and stroke.

Getting enough sleep will improve your memory, curb inflammation, sharpen attention, spur creativity, help you have a healthier weight, lower your stress, improve grades, and help you become a total winner.

One thing I want you to take away from this chapter is that change starts with a positive mindset, and to stick and grow with what you do change, is challenging. Sometimes simple meditation and being in alignment with yourself is all you need. Adding exercise to your meditation will make you feel and look younger. I find that people often get lost in their exercise regime because they do not know the kinds of exercises to do for quicker results. The following chapter gives great tips on how to effectively exercise for your body type.

Notes

Chapter 4

Great Tips for Impact and Exercise

Engaging in exercise that targets the whole body is a better way to burn calories, and eventually, shrinks the waistline. Processed food that contains hydrogenated oil, trans fat, and refined flour is known to construct fat growth in the midsection; alternatively, healthy monounsaturated fats, found in foods such as avocados, olive oil, and nuts, are recommended to improve fat loss.

Trust me; whether you are a beginner looking for guidance, or a top competitor, to lose belly fat fast, men's health recommends decreasing carbohydrate intake, eating more protein, exercising frequently, eating smaller portions at mealtime, combining cardiovascular exercise with weight lifting, and drinking lots of water. Keep the metabolism high by eating smaller meals throughout the day, rather than waiting long periods between large meals. Most exercises designed to target belly fat, such as crunches, are effective, intensity techniques, which is a body shocking principle that involves literally challenging the body by changing various aspects of your workout.

The body is amazingly adaptable and can accustom itself to workloads that would feel amazing. However, if you train the same way, the body will get used to a regular routine, and every intense training will yield less response than you expected. You can challenge your body by training with more weight than what you are used to. Also, doing more reps or sets speeds up your training. Cut down your rest time between sets, and do unfamiliar exercises. If you do your exercise in an unfamiliar order, make sure to use high intensity techniques. Change by itself tends to challenge the body, even if the unfamiliar workout is more demanding than your regular routine. On your fitness journey, you'll get to a point where you'll find it difficult to make additional progress without challenging your muscles into getting bigger, stronger, fuller, and harder, as well as with more definition.

Definition comes from using weights, yoga exercises, and running. There are various exercises one can do to define their body, and it does not always have to include being at the gym. Outdoor activities, like rock climbing, hiking, zip lining, or biking, can give definition to your body, as well as help limit excuses for not taking control of your health. Many institutions are affiliated with marathon programs, like the Boston Marathon, and the Breast Cancer Society, to help bring awareness to health and fitness. When a person does not exercise, they are minimizing their life span by the day.

In October of 2017, I had just walked away from my job after 6 years. I was excited that I had walked away from my job to go and work for my own company, full time. I was looking forward to being a full time entrepreneur. With little experience of owning a business, and not getting the right advice, I realized it was the wrong decision to have walked away from my previous job. After 3 months, I had to find a new job, because my business was not flourishing as I thought it would. The job that I found was physically demanding. I would often feel tired after working a 10-hour shift, which then limited me from going to the gym. I found different means of exercising while at work, I took advantage of the physically demanding part of my job by lifting boxes with techniques that would suffice my lack of workouts. Also, we would do stretches at various times during our shift.

The point I am making here is that there is no excuse for not exercising. For instance, if you work in an office building, there are different ways to get your body moving so that you would not have to be behind your desk all day feeling overworked. Some of the best ways are to take the stairs instead of the elevator, get up and stretch, go for a simple walk around the office, and find ways that can keep your body moving. Additionally, you can do simple calf raises while sitting in your chair at your desk, to keep the blood flowing. Also, reach for the ceiling with both arms, or with one after the other. You can open your arms to allow friction in movement. All of these basic simple stretches and exercises will help to reduce tension. These exercises are very basic and do not require rigorous movements, but they keep the blood flowing, hence releasing stress and anxiety.

Tips for Lower Back

A tip for people suffering from lower back pain is to first go on the lower back extension machine at your gym. This machine extends your back to help alleviate the pain. It helps release all the tense muscles, for better movement. My recommendation is to get a sponge mat, and roll on it for 15-25 minutes. Hanging stretches are also a great stretching method to help alleviate back pain. It will ease out any tension and will help stretch out your muscles. After this method of stretching, go into the sauna so that your tissues can open up—the heat of the sauna will help with the recovery process.

Tips for Losing Weight Without Going to the Gym

The best tip for losing weight, without going to the gym, is to fast once or twice a week, up to your comfortability. Another way is to have a fruit-blended smoothie in the morning; the nutrients of the fruits will keep you satisfied throughout the day. I will advise that you get a skipping rope and skip for 10-15 minutes, and do jumping jacks, which is also a good workout that does not have to be done at the gym. If you have a staircase at your house, I recommend that you run up and down it several times, or to your comfortability. Make sure, as you fast and exercise in the comfort your home, you are dehydrating your body with water. Another way of exercising at your home is by doing pushups, and you can speed walk around your neighborhood. Most people do not like to go to the gym because they feel self-conscious, or are intimidated by what others are doing, or they simply do not have the time to devote to a gym membership. My advice is to get a workout program to do at home, and follow it through. This breaks down any excuses for not exercising. The point I am making here is that there is always a way around achieving a healthier version of yourself.

Muscular Strength and Endurance

Movement requires the muscular system, which has the ability to know when to relax, produce force, and contract. It metabolically activates the tissues so high that it is able to respond to training stimuli. By doing the appropriate exercises, muscles become much larger and stronger; by not following the appropriate exercises, your muscles become weaker and smaller. This is an informational tool to let you know about the benefits of suitable strength for your body, and the recommended procedures for safe, effective, and efficient development.

Hydration

Use this information to assess if you are drinking enough water, or throughout the day to stay hydrated. The use of supplements may change the colour of your urine. Drink 8oz of water, eight times a day, to remain hydrated. Drinks that contain caffeine will cause you to dehydrate faster. Urine that is plentiful, odorless, and pale in colour generally indicates you are well hydrated. Dark (the colour of apple juice), strong smelling urine, and/or a small amount, could also be a sign of dehydration. It is important to make sure you are cutting out lots of carbonated drinks in your diet. Not only does it make you dehydrated, but the sugars in these drinks build more fat in your body. People have the misconception that drinks like Gatorade, Red Bull, or soda water will hydrate them enough throughout the day. These drinks have electrolytes to give you energy to be able to continue working out. The intake of high electrolyte drinks, without burning off some energy, rather makes you more lethargic.

Self-Determination

Having the desire to accomplish anything you set your mind to is the initiation of any debt of purpose. First, you need to have a burning desire, and set out to acquire that desired goal. Thomas Edison had the determination of creating the incandescent light bulb. He tried to perfect his creation with the determination to never fail, after trying over ten thousand times. If you do encounter any setbacks through your journey of fitness, you have to keep going, and that will fuel your self-determination. Sometimes, in the process of fitness, we are ridiculed because of other people's judgements and criticism, but that should not stop you from achieving what you have set in mind. Having self-determination blocks negative influences that might prohibit your process. Determination is the starting point to having any major achievements. If at any time you feel that you can't keep going, think about what always keeps you going.

Reject the Voices of the Past

A lot of people let their past haunt them, and that is because they have become accustomed to hearing those voices and living with it all the time. The past takes control of your thoughts; therefore, you find it difficult to let go of that mentality. Many women especially go through tremendous amounts of separation and turmoil by their spouses when there's a lot undue stress. This causes distress in the woman's life; they feel that whatever they contribute to making the family happy, is constantly being put down. Women are constantly being reminded of their flaws and their lack of self-worth. Those replaying voices are only temporary; you can control your thoughts. Through words of affirmation, and positive thinking, keep telling yourself you are the best person. Affirmations are pronouncements that you make to affirm that whatever you are going through will come to pass, and you will overcome every setback, regardless of what those circumstances are.

Men also go through having to overcome negative thoughts built in them by their spouses, loved ones, or simply just people in general. Never think that you aren't good enough. When you walk inside a gym for the first time, always remember that every other person in that gym might be going through the same thing. Size can break your confidence, but never give into those thoughts because it will hinder you from getting to where you want to be. People often walk into the gym feeling defeated because of their looks or whatever that might be happening in their personal lives, or as stated before, the judgements people might cast upon them. It actually helps if you go to a gym with a goal in mind, and with a positive attitude. Allow the judgements of other people to be your motivation in working harder, and do not allow the feeling to defeat or overshadow your mindset on being your best self. Always make sure that you stand firm in your truth; be confident and commit fully to whatever you do. By doing this, it will elevate your overall being, and help you deal with being around negative energy or people.

My experience came about many years ago, after meeting a female in the gym. I thought she was attractive enough, so I approached her. We built a friendship around similar interests in the gym. However, the more we hung out, the more I became attracted to her. As much as I liked her, she did not reciprocate the same feelings I had. She found fault with my height, and this was one of the many challenges I had to endure about being of average height. I always had aspirations of being an underwear model, but I was always told I couldn't because I did not fit the image of being a model, due to my height. People would make fun of me and call me midget, because I was short; and other people never saw me as their equal.

I experienced most of these challenges when I was younger, but I did not realize I would have to endure more of it as I became older. I had to work hard on my confidence so that it overshadowed my average height. When you are confident, other flaws that might be visible disappear instantly, and people start to know you for who you truly are, other than for your external features. One morning, after I got ready for church, I felt confident in what I was wearing, so I decided I was going to take some pictures. After taking the pictures and observing the photos, I started to believe what everyone was saying about my height. On my way to church, I was thinking to myself and wondering why I was allowing the voices of other people to affect me. I had to tell myself to snap out of it. When I got to church and saw the guest pastor, who was of average height himself, it became a confirmation that I could be powerful as well— what stood out to me was that he spoke so eloquently and powerfully. This resonated with me because I realized that people of average height can be powerful. It changed my mindset on how I should be looking at myself. People like Dr. Martin Luther King, Kevin Hart, and Tom Cruise, to name a few, never allowed their lack of height to stop them from achieving greatness.

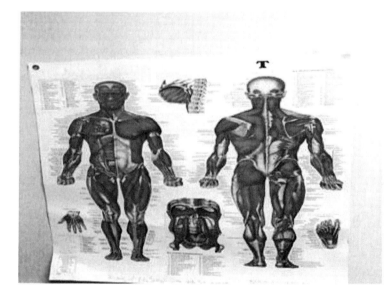

This chapter is all about the tips on working on a specific body part you want to improve on. It will also help you find ways to gain muscular strength and endurance, nourishing your body through hydration. It's important to be determined in everything you do, and this chapter stresses the importance of being self- determined, as well as rejecting the voices of the past. As we age, we will sometimes have to deal with chronic conditions, and the next chapter sets ways for you in battling chronic diseases.

Notes

Chapter 5

Remedy for an Enlarged Liver, Testosterone, Inflammation, and Other Chronic Diseases

What is the remedy for an enlarged liver due to visceral fat? Eating a healthy diet that focuses on losing weight helps to reduce belly fat. Usually, this means that visceral fat is lost at the same time. Increasing fiber helps to reduce visceral fat. Exercising also increases the calories burned during the day, to help individuals achieve their weight loss goals. Most people do at least half an hour of exercise, five or more days per week. Practically any activity that increases the heart rate counts as exercise. People who sleep between six and seven hours per night find it easier to reduce their visceral fat levels. Those who sleep more than eight hours, or less than five hours per night, generally see an increase in belly fat overtime.

Stress is a part of life. Learning to handle stress reduces its effect on health. Spending time with family and friends, as well as doing exercise and meditation, helps to reduce stress. If self-help steps to reduce stress do not help, the individual often benefits from the professional help of a counselor.

According to Willie Tabor, a Facebook friend who sent me a message on an article I posted, and I quote, "I loved your first presentation on men over forty. It was awesome. Visceral fat was one of the issues we had been discussing at my men's church group, during 2016. I had visited my doctor several times, until my urologist discovered that my urine was causing severe infection. I had a prompt procedure done in June 2016. I had to discontinue, given my testosterone level. It dropped from 438 to 82. OMG, I was dragging my tail. In January, my urologist resumed my injections. Now, my testosterone level is 843—what a difference! My diet usually consists of salads, fruits, chicken, and fish. Very seldom do I eat peanut butter, juice, or anything with preservatives for breakfast. The video was very informative. I worked out this morning at Lifetime Fitness, for forty-five minutes. The mucus started coming up, and I was getting very tired. I will be back tomorrow, and until I build up."

What are some symptoms of an enlarged liver? An enlarged liver, or hepatomegaly, occurs when the liver swells above its normal size. According to WebMD, an enlarged liver is usually a symptom of an underlying condition, such as a viral infection, or certain types of hepatitis cysts and tumors; however, there are many other conditions that could cause the liver to swell. Additional causes include specific medication, toxins, certain metabolic and autoimmune diseases, and even an excess buildup of fat and protein in the liver. An enlarged liver may also be caused by problems in blood flow, including congestive heart failure, or hepatic vein thrombosis, which is a blockage in the veins of the liver. Having an enlarged liver is a dangerous condition that could lead to liver failure. In simple terms, fatty liver disease means the accumulation of fat in the cells of the liver.

It is normal to have fat in the liver, but when there is more than ten percent of fat, it can be considered fatty liver disease. A buildup of fat in the liver makes it vulnerable to further injury that can cause inflammation and scarring. There are two types of fatty liver disease: alcohol-induced and nonalcoholic. This condition hits close to home, as my own stepfather passed away from drinking lots of alcohol for many years. This condition was very evident, as you could tell from the pigmentation of his skin. Oftentimes, you would hear my mother tell him that drinking alcohol in such great quantities would one day be his demise. I have watched his skin change, where small areas would break out to larger spots. This took a toll on his body and the severe condition that his liver was undergoing. The main cause behind alcoholic-induced fatty liver is excessive alcohol consumption, and for non-alcoholic fatty liver, fat builds up in the liver for reasons unrelated to alcohol. Apart from excessive alcohol consumption, risk factors for fatty liver diseases include high blood cholesterol, high blood pressure, obesity, type two diabetes, viral hepatitis, rapid weight loss, and malnutrition.

1) Apple cider vinegar is one of the best remedies for fatty liver diseases. It helps to get rid of fat accumulated in and around the liver, and promotes weight loss.

The best way to alleviate this problem is by visiting your doctor if this symptom arises. The doctor can perform several tests, a CT scan, or even a liver biopsy. According to WebMD, once the underlying condition is discovered, the doctor can then begin treatment. Your liver works harder to filter nearly everything that enters your body, including harsh toxins and impurities. In case your liver goes through scarring, it is one of the organs that can repair itself and grow new tissues. One recommendation is to drink lots of water to help the liver flush the excess toxins that the liver is undergoing. Water helps to flush and minimize any long-term conditions that may be of cause to your body. The liver is like the gatekeeper to the body. It prevents unwanted toxins that may end up going to the kidneys.

It is important to ensure that you are visiting your doctor to find out if there's any unwanted conditions that the liver may be going through. One way that you can tell when your liver is working overtime is if you are having burning sensations. Fatty liver is also caused from blood sugar levels. Whatever additional difficulties that the liver may undergo, the kidneys would be the supporter in preventing other unwanted problems. The kidneys are able to work as a second gatekeeper in preventing other unwanted substances. However, the kidneys should be treated with great caution, to prevent kidney failure. Should the kidneys encounter any challenges, there are no supplements to remedy this cause.

There are two ways in which the body goes through bowel movements after the liver passes on unwanted nutrients to the kidneys. Having a healthy liver is very important to not cause the body to break down. Drinking lots of water in the morning after waking up will allow for proper bowel movements, because water pushes all the toxins down. Taking small sips of water throughout the day makes it easier for your body to absorb it. Water will pass through the body because it has nowhere to store it. The complex carbohydrates, like in vegetables, will help slow down the absorption process, or to space it out. When your blood sugar goes very high, you are able to store a lot of energy into fat, and that's why we need to not overeat.

Sources WebMD,
Testmaxnutrition.com

Men's Health

"About twenty to thirty percent of your daily calories should come from fat, and not just those heart-healthy monounsaturated fats found in olive oil. Saturated fats contain cholesterol, which is a crucial processor to testosterone production. Consuming enough calories prevents the body from slowing testosterone production as a reaction to perceived starvation."

According to Nutri Search, written by Lyle McWilliams, the more researchers probe systemic inflammation, the more they expose its links to other disease processes. Many researchers now believe that low grade systemic inflammation is the basis for accelerated aging and the development of degenerative diseases. Chronic inflammation is also an underlying cause of excess body fat and the inability to lose weight, and it may be the important missing link in the current obesity epidemic. It is associated with the onset of diabetes. A recent study on inflammation and type two diabetes provides support for a common inflammatory, and this is for both AD and diabetes. Diabetes has steeply elevated levels of inflammation, and many individuals commonly suffer from both diseases.

In patients with AD, inflammation of the brain tissues increases the production of soluble beta-amyloid protein and its conversion to insoluble amyloid fibrils. Accumulation of these harmful protein fibrils is closely associated with the deterioration of brain function. Moreover, because of the molecular structure, the presence of beta-amyloid fibrils can overstimulate the immune system, leading to increased inflammation. In type 2 diabetics, amyloid protein deposits, similar to those found in the Alzheimer's brain, can form in the pancreas, knocking out of action the cells responsible for the production of insulin. Chronically elevated levels of insulin and blood sugar, common to those suffering from metabolic syndrome (a prediabetes state, characterized by increased insulin resistance and oxidative stress), trigger inflammatory events similar to those in AD that lead to the accumulation of these harmful protein plaques.

Chronic inflammation of the gastrointestinal tract can have far-reaching consequences, including the inability to absorb essential nutrients and the development of osteoporosis. Patients with inflammatory bowel disorder, a chronic inflammatory condition of the gut, demonstrate an inordinately high risk of osteoporosis. Inflammation of the specialized cells lining the digestive tract appears to contribute to an imbalance in bone destroying inflammatory proteins in the blood. This, in turn, leads to bone mineral loss and even greater systemic inflammation. Inflammation also promotes several types of cancer.

Stress Control

According to *Men's Health*, anxiety is normal, but overwhelming worry is disabling. Anxiety disorders are the most common mental health problem, affecting 40 million U.S. adults. They range from generalized anxiety disorder, to panic disorder, to obsessive compulsive disorder. Anxiety about performance disables us with worry, phobias, and panic. Positivity is a key test of mental health. Your stress response is a gatekeeper of mental health. A brain structure, called the *amygdala*, can trigger a cascade of stress hormones. Chronic stress can cause inflammation, and it ups your rate of brain shrinkage. Activation of the GABA neurons in the amygdala can interrupt memory, decision making, and cognitive abilities. Men often respond to anxiety with passivity. As soon as you finish watching a TV show that caused your heart rate to be increased, your anxiety will resurface.

Think of relaxation as another muscle that needs regular exercise. If the idea of meditation makes you anxious, focus on relearning how to breathe. Lie face up, with one hand on your belly. As you inhale, feel it rise; as you exhale, feel it drop. Deep belly breathing helps lower heart rate, blood pressure, and other physiological manifestations of stress. People I speak to, talk about their ways of stress fighting through the power of exercise, being outdoors, and deepening their spiritual practices.

The 7 Types of Cancer

Drinking and smoking equals a greater risk of cancer. There are seven types of cancers caused by alcohol consumption.

Bowel Cancer – which is also known as colorectal cancer. It starts in the colon and rectum. This type of cancer is more common in elderly individuals who are 60 years and above, but it is also important to know that it can happen at any time. Some of the symptoms are changes in bowel movements, blood in stool, and abdominal pain.

Breast Cancer – is the common amongst women. The symptoms of breast cancer include a change in the breast shape or size, or a lump or thickening in the breast or the armpit. Make sure to pay attention to any fluid that might come out of the breast, or redness, irritation, or skin changes. The risk of alcohol-related cancers increases more if you consume alcohol daily.

Oral Cancer – is when your mouth and throat are irritated from consuming large amounts of alcohol. This can cause dryness, bad breath, and changing color of the teeth. There can also be lesions inside the mouth, as well as swelling. Be sure to visit your dentist within 2 weeks if you see any of these symptoms occur.

Laryngeal Cancer – Drinking alcohol causes a higher than average risk of developing cancer in the larynx. The chemicals contained in alcohol pass over the top of the larynx as you swallow. Compared to non-drinkers, the risk of developing laryngeal cancer is more than twice as high for heavy drinkers.

Oesophageal cancer – The symptoms include difficulty swallowing, persistent indigestion or heartburn, pain in your throat or behind your breastbone. Lifestyle factors, such as obesity, smoking, and alcohol, cause 9 out of 10 oesophageal cancers. This cancer starts in the cells of the skin. Even light drinking increases the risk.

Oropharyngeal cancer (upper throat) – The upper throat is the area behind the nose and mouth, which leads to the top of the esophagus and windpipe. Upper throat cancer is caused by the consumption of large amounts of alcohol. Thirty percent of upper throat cancers are caused by drinking.

Liver Cancer – As we discussed earlier, this is the well-known cancer that has a long-term effect on the liver when a lot of alcohol is consumed. Long-term drinking leads to cirrhosis, whereby the liver is repeatedly damaged, and scar tissue is built up. It also damages the DNA in the liver cells.

Chronic conditions are inevitable as we become older. We must take good care of our bodies now so that when we get older, we won't have to experience much. Some of the remedies listed above will definitely reduce the risk of experiencing chronic conditions, in addition to exercising. The next chapter stresses more on taking good care of your body by living a healthy lifestyle. Living a healthy lifestyle doesn't mean starving yourself or overworking your body. It's doing what is right for your body, and the way you see progression.

Notes

Chapter 6

Once a Man Twice a Child

As a young man, I always heard my grandparents say, "Once a man twice a child." I had no clue what they were talking about, but as I got older, I became fully aware of what they meant. When you are born, you're in the custody of your parents, because they are caring for you. They provide your necessities to live. The same can be said for senior citizens, who may end up having to be taken care of by a caregiver if they end up in a nursing home. This similar situation also happened to both of my grandparents, where they were being cared for by their grandchild. That leads me to understand that one has to take good care of their health in order to live a healthy and long life, even if you end up having a caregiver in a nursing home. Most people do not end up realizing this until the later years in their life. It has become an epidemic in whether or not they have the resources to visit their doctor on a frequent basis. While living in Jamaica, this kind of lifestyle was evident because health care was expensive, or the individual simply did not understand the importance of the improvement of their health. Finding out any health complication at an early stage will prevent or reduce the risk of long-term problems.

The problem is that we take our bodies for granted. We just assume that we will be healthy, and that we don't have to do anything to guarantee that we stay healthy; but when we get sick, or have an accident, we realize we can't do the things for our bodies, so we regret not taking care of it. Sometimes it is sickness or adversity that brings us to the pursuit of fitness. The reality of our fitness and health is that we were born with the opportunity to be everything we can be, through thousands of years of evolution. Nature has made it easy to do what it takes in order to feel good. Give 160 hours a week, and your body will function fantastically. People often ask me if all this is true, and then, if so, why is it that in our culture most people are so terribly unfit? We have to consider that the unfitness epidemic, with its chronic anxiety and feelings of unease, is really only a blip on the human radar screen of history. It's only been about 60 years, as our ancestors were very physical.

Our society has evolved over time from what humans traditionally are used to doing. Our ancestors had to hunt with their bare hands, as there were no tools available to do the types of things we do in these recent times. People don't think they have to do something physical in their everyday lives. Our evolutionary concept of learning physical activity hasn't caught up, but there has been a massive shift amongst the Western world, with millennials understanding the importance of fitness. There is a phenomenon about proper fitness programs, for a healthier longer life.

Over 2/3 of our population does not get enough exercise. Currently, only 13 percent of the total population of North America is working out at a fitness club. I think the time is coming when people will become smart enough to realize that this is what they have to do, to discover that it doesn't have to be hard, and that it is actually very easy and fun. What happens when you don't exercise is that you hasten your death. While you're chasing your death, you lower your quality of life. In order to get people to the state of looking good and feeling good, we, in the fitness industry, have to find ways to take the fear out of exercise. The concept behind most people not attending the gym is that they feel they that will be judged. We need to create a no-judgement zone, in order for clients to feel comfortable when they decide to join the gym or a fitness club. I can remember walking into a gym at a different location, and there were athletes competing for a bodybuilding competition. I was intimidated a little when I compared myself to these muscle builders, who have rightfully worked hard to get to their stage in fitness. Now,

17 years later, I have received numerous amounts of messages on social media, or in person, from individuals who feel intimidated by my fitness appearance—they would complement me on the way my body looks, and express their desire to achieve my fitness level.

Images of perfection, athleticism, and fitness have to go. These images have become so prevalent in our society because the extremes attract attention. It's not news when they show a picture of several types of women who have children and are all within 20 percent of their ideal body weight, and are comfortable with themselves. They will tell you that there are thousands of ways to strengthen your biceps. It's not that complicated. What you do is really easy, and you don't need to know 1000 ways to have the kind of body you want. The only thing you need to know is that fitness is a lifestyle that does not require a lot of work. Ninety percent of your fitness goals is what you do at home. Eating right, getting proper sleep, and reducing stress levels is all a part of an overall fitness program.

Going to the gym for a mere 1½ hours is just the icing on the cake. The most complicated pieces of equipment are barbells and dumbbells, but you don't need to use them. Most of the advertisements surrounding exercise equipment puts emphasis on them, but you never have to touch one. Your own body weight is a tool by itself, which you can use to build a healthy and happier you. It's also true that some people join a fitness club because, if they discover they have some athletic talent, they will run marathons to perfect their goals, or play basketball, participate in track and field, go hiking, and or do other fitness programs.

If the statistics continue to indicate that 70 percent of people don't participate in extracurricular exercise, I can perceive that our own health may decrease in several years. We will then begin to pay the price for lack of activity; on the other hand, if we get 30 to 40 percent of people being active, then that will create an enormous jump, and positive health outcomes. If things continue as they are now, I see a huge increase in overweight people dying younger, with a great cost to health and social systems. The people constantly putting their health first do not have to worry so much about health costs. Those who are healthy would not have to take many sick days, their productivity increases, and they are more likely to have a positive outlook on life, regardless of any circumstances or challenges. Possibly, in the future, we may see an increase in individuals who pressure the government to implement measures to combat laziness, or the government will implement programs with incentives to get people, who are lazy, to become more active.

Let's get back to feeling good; what other things can we say about fitness that make us feel good? Even sex is better, and your body, your mind, and your soul will feel and look better. It turns your partner on more, so you feel more at ease to be touched. The full physical capacity will last longer, and there will be a greater ability for sustained pleasure; therefore, there is no need for sexual enhancements like Viagra. Exercise is also a great method to improve sperm count or libido. Studies have shown that exercise elevates mood. A lot of emotional problems are caused by feelings of loss of control. If you are feeling bad about yourself, the first step towards getting control is doing what you innately know is right, and that may be a physical activity. It's hard describing in exact words, but you know when you feel good. Health problems, such as diabetes, cardiovascular disease, or high blood pressure, will continue to increase if people do not understand the importance of their health problems.

Health problems related to unhealthy lifestyles are already a cost to our health system. Everyone talks about having a perfect weight, and we are obsessed in this culture, because we are tied to our sense of self-worth and self-esteem. People go to great lengths to do something about their weight. What do people mean when they say they want the perfect weight? They mean that when they walk down the street, people will cast admiring glances at them, and every photographer in the world will want to put them on the cover of *Men's Health*, or other related news tabloids. This can be said about several celebrities. It's about how you look that gets you the most attention. Your clothes will fit you better, and you will have clothing companies recruiting you for marketing purposes.

When it comes to weight, the influence of public media is insidious. Ninety-nine percent of the population simply cannot look like those models and celebrities. Very often, when you see a movie star or a person in front of you, you find out that they don't look nearly so perfect in the flesh as they do in the magazine. We find ourselves obsessing with perpetual thinness, and that is the current cultural idea that often promotes negative results for health and self-esteem. We lose sight of the fact that different tiers of history have had different images of attractiveness. Some eras have valued the full-figured body, but we need to learn to distinguish what a good weight is, which is possible for anyone. We need to know the difference between what a good weight is, and what is overweight. We need to understand that our body weight is an aspect of our total overall health; therefore, ideal weight is when our bodies function at their best. People who spend a lot of time on the couch encounter challenges with their health.

Because we take our bodies for granted, we tend to lose the desire to begin to improve them, because we are used to our comfort zone. We have become accustomed to having the microwavable way of doing things, so we lose the demand to put in effort when it comes to physical activity. The chapter that follows is more of a personal story about the men I worked with while I was in the manufacturing industry. It will give you more of an insight into my character, and how I took the initiative in the well-being of my other coworkers.

Notes

Notes

Chapter 7

Men on the Assembly Line

After arriving in Canada, in March 2011, the common thing for one to do would be to get a job. Not having a career that can easily put you in the field of work that you are coming from, or have trained in, makes you feel less competent. I found that I was one of those people that would have to start from the bottom up. One of the easiest places I could find that would give me that chance was in a manufacturing industry. On August 8th, 2011, I started to work in one of Canada's prominent bedding companies, and I quickly realized that this was going to be it for some time, as I needed to start earning an income. As I walked the floor of the manufacturing area, it was clear to me that men were not very fit or somewhat taking care of themselves.

Lunchtime was the perfect place to observe the way the men were eating, as we were separated from the women at lunch time, and for the most part of the day. There was a wide range of age of people on the factory floor, and some, I think, were in their late 60s. A wide range of races was also very evident, and I thought to myself that this was a good balance of individuals for me to gather information from. As the months and the years continued, I observed their eating patterns, which were not good. Some, I assumed, were set in their ways because of their age range. The men would ask me about my physical appearance and if I was a bodybuilder.

I was curious to know about their own health patterns. As I gathered information by talking to them, I found out how often they would visit their doctor, and also if they got their prostate checked.

Some were open to answering the questions, and others were not so open, because talking about getting a prostate exam or going to the doctor is sometimes not a comfortable topic, especially amongst African Americans and Caucasians. They would say they were not comfortable going to the doctor to have him insert his or her finger in their anus. This was common amongst many Jamaicans, as my grandfather died from prostate cancer.

As a young boy, I would hear my grandfather groan from the pain he was feeling from his testicles; there was a lot of swelling. The first indication of prostate complications is a burning sensation in the penis. My grandmother would say to me, "Don't have lots of pepper because it will give you *stoppigawater* (a blockage of the penis)." From then on, I was reluctant to eat pepper. I would observe, on the washroom floor around the urinal, that there would be excess stains, and my best guess was that the constant smoking, and other situations, had caused this build-up. Some of the men that I spoke to would often go to visit their doctor because they knew the severity of the risk of having prostate issues.

After many months of having conversations with these men, and observing how they eat, I requested a meeting with the human resource person, to discuss my findings and to see what we could do to implement measures to better improve the health conditions of these men. She instructed me to go to the health and safety manager, who thought this was a very good idea as she had just started a program where in which there were monthly newsletters on various topics. Also, during our monthly town hall meetings, there were discussions in regard to the importance of getting medical checks and prostate exams. One other way these men were educated on the importance of getting their prostate checked was through videos and documentaries on the steps that need to be taken to prevent these problems. These findings were published in all locations. In my experience, because there was high demand on the job, I was not able to use the washroom when I wanted to; and I believe it was the same experience for these men, which is why most of these men have prostate problems and bladder infections.

According to *Men's Health* magazine, "understanding the new concept of energy flux may be the key to understanding the secret of weight loss." Early researchers, from way back in the 1950s, suggested that people who move the least may consume more calories than they expend. The more exercise a person gets, the easier it could be to avoid weight gain, but something else happens at the extremes—something scientists still don't fully understand. Paradoxically, the higher the numbers (calories in, calories out), the leaner you may be, and the easier it may be to control fat. It was borne out by a three-year *American Journal of Clinical Nutrition* study of teenagers, published in 2016. The scientists found that teens who ate a lot of calories, reduced their body fat percentage over 3 years, while those who ate little and burned little, gained fat. This is despite the fact that teens in the *high flunk* group were eating several hundred more calories a day than they needed to maintain their weight, at the start of the study, while the *low flunk* teens were eating below maintenance. The combination of high intake and high expenditure was somehow more powerful than either variables in isolation, making them leaner than they should have been.

Battling in the fat wars and being overweight is not a comfortable or healthy way to live. It is too much for a particular body type, especially when it shortens the length of life and severely compromises your sense of well-being. Why do we get overweight? Quite simply by not doing enough physical activity and eating too much. In previous generations, our ancestors did a lot of physical work, which included gathering and hunting to get through the day to survive. As our society develops, we have more labor saving devices, such as tractors and washing machines; and the workplace becomes more sedentary, and no longer has the benefit of the physical demands of activity. Also, take into account that the average age in our society is becoming older.

Buns of Steel

Notes

Notes

Chapter 8

Effective Stretching Methods

Stretching is one of the most neglected areas of a workout. If you watch a cat as it wakes from a nap and gets to its feet, you would see that the cat immediately stretches its whole body to its full length, readying every muscle, tendon, and ligament for instant and brutal action. The cat knows instinctively that stretching primes its strength. Muscles, tendons, ligaments, and joint structures are flexible, but they can stiffen, limiting your range of motion and the ability to contract muscle fiber. That is why stretching before you train allows you to train harder. Stretching makes your training safer as you extend your muscle fully under the pull of a weight—they can easily be pulled too far if your range of motion is limited. Overextension of tendons or ligaments can result in a strain or sprain, and can seriously interfere with your workout schedule. But if you stretch the areas involved first, the body will adjust as heavy resistance pulls on the structure involved.

Flexibility will also increase if the various exercises are done properly. A muscle can contract, but it cannot stretch itself; it has to be stretched by the pull of an opposing muscle. When you train through a full range of motion, you will increase your flexibility, but that isn't enough. Muscle contracted against heavy resistance tends to shorten with the effort. Therefore, I recommend stretching in order to allow you to train harder and more safely, as well as stretching after you train. To stretch out those tight and tired muscles, you can prepare for your workout by doing any number of the standard stretching exercises, as follows. You might also consider taking a yoga or stretching class, although many fitness athletes feel that this extra effort devoted to flexibility is not as necessary as doing your workout. Stretching allows the body to feel more flexible.

Stretching Exercises

Side bend:

The purpose of this exercise is to stretch the oblique muscles, as well as other muscles on the side of the torso.

Execution: Stand upright, with feet slightly more than shoulder width apart; raise your right arm over your head, and bend slowly to the left. Letting your left hand slide down your thigh, bend as far as you can, and hold this position for about 35 seconds; return to stretching position and then repeat with the opposite side.

Forward bends:

The purpose of this exercise is to stretch the hamstrings and lower back.

Execution: Stand upright, with feet together; bend forward to take hold of the back of your legs, as far down as possible—knees, calves, or ankles—and pull gently with your arms, bringing in your arms as close as possible to your legs in order to stretch the lower back and hamstrings to their limit. Hold this position for 35–65 seconds, and then relax. Place one foot or ankle on a support; keeping your other leg straight, bend forward along the raised leg and take hold of it as far down as possible—knee, calf, ankle, or foot—and pull gently to get the maximum stretch in the hamstring. Hold for about 35 seconds, relax, and then repeat the movement, using the other leg.

Lunges:

The purpose of this exercise is to stretch the inner thighs, hamstrings, and glutes.

Execution: Stand upright; move one leg forward, then bend that knee, coming down so that the knee of your trailing leg touches the floor; place your hand on either side of your front foot to get the maximum stretch of the inner thigh. From this position, straighten your forward leg and lock your knee; straighten the hamstring at the back of the leg. Bring the other knee forward and lower yourself to the floor again; repeat this movement, first straightening the leg, then coming down to the floor again. Stand upright once more, step forward with the opposite, and repeat the stretching procedure.

Feet apart-seated forward bends:

The purpose of this exercise is to stretch the hamstrings and lower back.

Execution: Sit on the floor, with legs straight and wide apart; bend forward and touch the floor with your hands, as far in front of you as possible.

Hold this position for a few seconds, and then walk your hands over one leg; then grip it as far down as possible—knee, calf, or ankle—then pull gently on your leg to get the maximum stretch of your hamstring and lower back. Hold this position for about 35 seconds; then walk your hands over the other leg and repeat.

Inner thigh stretches:

The purpose of this exercise is to stretch the inner thighs.

Execution: Sit on the floor and draw your feet towards you, so the soles are touching.

Take hold of your feet; then pull them as close to the groin as possible. Relax your legs and drop towards the floor, stretching the inner thighs. Press down on your knees with your elbows to get a more complete stretch. Hold for 35–65 seconds, and then relax.

Quadriceps stretches:

The purpose of this exercise is to stretch the front of the thighs.

Execution: Kneel on the floor, and separate your feet enough so that you can sit between them. Put your hands on the floor behind you and lean back as far as possible, feeling the stretch in the quadriceps. Those who are less flexible will be able to lean back a little; those who are very flexible will be able to lay back on the floor. Hold this position for 35–65 seconds, and then relax.

Stretches are a very important method for production. Many companies have a regular routine in their programs to enable better flexibility and greater production. One company in particular is

Amazon. At Amazon, they are trained to stretch for greater efficiency and best practice, to reduce injury towards the body. Some stretches include: hand movements, where you exercise the hands; squatting properly, to alleviate pain in the waist and the back; and bending the knees for proper lifting, and to avoid injury from heavy lifting. This practice is universal to all Amazon locations. Therefore, this practice in stretching shows that there is a need to stretch before exercise, as it helps to prepare you for what you will be encountering. Be safe in your stretching, practice proper posture, and maintain deep breathing to better engage the body.

Spinal twist:

The purpose of this exercise is to increase the rotational range of motion of the torso, and to stretch the outer thighs.

Execution: Sit on the floor; with legs extended in front of you, bring your right knee up and twist around so that your left elbow rests on the outside of the upraised knee. Place your right hand on the floor, and continue to twist to the right as far as possible. Twist to the extreme of your range of motion, and hold for 30 seconds; lower your right knee, bring up your left, and repeat the motion with the other side.

Seated Row:

The purpose of this exercise is to develop the back and create a lat spread.

Execution: Sit with legs pushing forward; grip a T bar, and pull forward as close as possible to the belly button. Keep the abs tight, while releasing to the starting position.

Most people tend to forget to stretch before and after exercising because they do not feel that it's a necessity to exercising. Stretching is one of the essential parts of exercising because it helps to relax and elongate your muscles in order for you to exercise at your max capacity. This chapter also helps you understand that stretching will help minimize any injuries and keep you in balance. Oftentimes, we do not fathom the importance of being fit. We tend to go about our usual routines when we are exercising. Once you find your rhythm and maintain it, make sure to stay on that track and keep improving on it. This will help you understand the importance of fitness.

Buns of Steel

Notes

Notes

Chapter 9

Understanding the Importance of Fitness

There could not be life without fitness; everything we do has a great influence on our movements. All it takes is to incorporate 160 minutes in a week. It does not matter what you do; simply walking is good. Going up the stairs is more effective than taking an elevator. I have found that this has helped me so much to reduce stress, just by going up two flights of stairs. I lived in a building that had 23 flights of stairs, and I would often run up and down those flights. If you live in a building or work in an office, using the stairs is also a form of exercising. I would often go up the stairs with my laundry, just to get an additional amount of exercise. In past times, because vehicles were not as prominent as they are today, walking was the only way of getting to where you wanted to go.

There is a great amount of admiration that is often shown to individuals who pursue fitness. Athletes live a life that is built on fitness. The four-time Olympic champion, Usain Bolt, is a prime example of a person who faced many challenges that could have prevented him from being the best runner; but instead, it motivated him to be the greatest of all time. One cannot be a great athlete without overcoming hurdles in the process. It's not about where you start but where you finish; along the way, there would be many challenges to face. Fitness always seems to be that one thing that you could always rely on to give you that boost of energy to keep you going. I have met and had many conversations with individuals in the gym, and whenever I spoke to them, relieving stress seemed to be one of the main topics that always seemed to come up. What seemed to be the number one factor in their stress levels was having to work long hours—not only did it affect them, but it also affected their families. Fitness became the only way to alleviate their stress level.

When you exercise, endorphins are released, and they interact with the receptors of the brain that reduce pain, stress, and fatigue. It makes you feel like you are on a high; hence, this is why you feel much more positive and happier after your workout. Another important topic that came up in my conversations with these individuals was the progression of their fitness level. Most said they gained a lot more strength, and they have found different methods of exercise that work best for them, as well as workout supplements that help boost their endurance. Fasting also helps the body to get rid of the bacteria that builds up. Lots of the foods we eat are processed foods, so sometimes fasting at our own discretion helps to metabolize our system again. It's a recalibration for our immune system, which in the long run helps us to not give in to our food cravings. When we crave foods, we normally crave things that contain high sugar, carbohydrates, and saturated fats. Depending on your body type, you might need certain foods more than others.

Learning Your Body Type

According to the Arnold Schwarzenegger encyclopedia, there are three types of body types. There is the ectomorph, mesomorph, and endomorph. An ectomorph tends to be lean and long; they have difficulty building muscle, and therefore must put in extra effort to gain muscle mass. In order for them to gain muscle, they must learn to train intensely and make every set count. In 2013, I was a novice competitor in the International Drug Free Association (IDFA). I was what you would consider an ectomorph. I weighed 182 lbs. prior to my competition. I went through a 12-week diet program to gain the measured weight of 152 lbs., as a novice competitor. I had to change my diet; I had to abstain from large amounts of carbohydrates, and I had to eat more protein. I had to train intensely by doing increasing increments of cardio, and I had to build more defined muscles in areas where I was lacking. I basically had to have the body of a mesomorph. I advanced in two rounds and was 3rd in the last round.

Mesomorphs are muscular and well built. They have a large bone structure and a naturally athletic physique. They are naturally strong and the perfect body type for body building competitions. They gain so easily, so they do not have to do much or over train. A workout consists of 16–20 sets per body part, and they do not need to have lots of rest between workout sets.

An endomorph is bigger in structure; they have high body fat, and they tend to store most of that fat. The best recommendation for endomorphs is to have a higher proportion of high sets, with many repetitions. A low calorie diet is essential, with vitamins and minerals.

Notes

Chapter 10

A Life of Rewarding and Fulfilling Moments

I was approached by an expert in personal training and bodybuilding, who thought I looked good enough to compete in bodybuilding. I had little experience in competitive sports. Even though I had gone to several competitions, I did not understand the true amount of work it takes for one to compete professionally. Soon, I became aware of what I was going up against, after my trainer outlined to me the 12 different techniques of posing, which I would have to practice in order to be competitive. Some of the 12 poses consisted of front lateral, side lateral, front double bicep, side triceps, and rear delts. Quickly, I got used to the names and techniques of the poses. I got eager to learn and to go through the process of transforming my body, and that was a rewarding and fulfilling moment for me. This process lasted for 12 weeks in total, and we trained 3 times a week.

In the 6th week, I started to see massive improvements in my physical appearance. My poses were starting to look more perfected. My diets were very strict because I had to maintain my overall physique, as there were only 4 weeks left before the competition. This could be said about many individuals who were preparing for competition just the way I did. We all shared great moments, as it was the first time experiencing this for some people, including myself. Three days prior to the competition, I got so thin that my partner became scared about whether or not I would be able to compete. However, the loss of weight was a part of the process. I needed to weigh in at my desired weight class. The day before the competition, we all had to go get weighed with the organizers, to make sure we were competition ready, in our desired weight class. I measured in at 152 lbs., as a novice lightweight. At that moment, there was lots of excitement amongst the athletes, because we all had a chance to see who we were going up against. I was nervous because I had never experienced this before. After we all got an opportunity to see each other, I had my last meal, which was doughnuts, at 12am, to sustain me throughout the next day.

My trainer encouraged me to not focus on the other competitors and not to be discouraged. He motivated me that I could place in the top 3, because he knew that I was capable of achieving it. I couldn't sleep for most of the night because I was excited but still had doubts about my ability to place in the top three. After 4 hours of sleep, I went for a long run to clear my mind and to prepare my thoughts about what I was going to experience. At 7:30am in the morning, my trainer arrived, and he was beaming with excitement at the possibility of me placing in the top three. I arrived at the location of the competition, with much fanfare of the other athletes. There were other individuals who brought their coaches and loved ones to support them. I arrived in the holding area where all the competitors were gathered, and at that moment, it became real that I was about to undertake a life-changing experience.

For anyone who has spent a great amount of time perfecting their body, they would have full knowledge of the grueling experience. While I was backstage, we were all getting that last pump in to look our best on stage. There were urine tests done to ensure that everyone was drug free. We had to put on tanning cream so that the muscles would be more defined and visible. It was now time for the audience to arrive and the competitors to take their place. We had to go through a process of elimination. When I got on stage, there were about 400 people in the audience, and I could see the reflection of the light on my skin. I was nervous, but I could hear my friends in the audience yelling out my number, which was 11, and that was an indication for me to step up my game.

At this time, the other competitors were going through their process of elimination. After this process of elimination, we went backstage again, myself and the other athletes, and we started to pump up again; it was time for the final round, which was also when the judges would make their decision. We were called to the sideline, as it was close to the time for us to be on stage for the announcement of the winners. Based on my coach's experience, he believed I could be placed in the top three. We were finally called on stage, and we went through the final procedure where we were asked to do a posedown. The posedown is where all the athletes show off their best poses at the same time. This helps the judges pick out the best poses for the top three.

It was time for the winners to be announced. My name was called first, and I was very excited. The other winners were announced, and we posed for photo ops. I could still hear my support system cheering me on. That was a gratifying moment. I thought to myself that all my hard work rewarded me 3rd place out of nine other athletes. After the top three were mentioned, we got off stage. I had the opportunity to speak to the judges and get their feedback, and talk about the reason why I was not placed higher. Their feedback was that my legs were not defined enough compared to the other two winners. They commended me on my poses and my upper body. After the competition was over, I showed gratitude to my coach and my support system.

A couple of days after the competition, my coach and I assessed what we could improve on. We started a program on how to improve my overall physique, as we were looking forward to compete again at the pro athletic level. The novice competition was the stepping stone to all the other major bodybuilding competitions in Canada. However, as the months went by, I was not able to continue my training regime because many other life changing experiences happened. I still continued to train as often as I could, to maintain my physical appearance. Even though I did not compete in the pro athletic level, I went as a spectator, and I was filled with memories.

My advice to anyone who wants to compete in bodybuilding is to first of all take into consideration the rule in life: you are a competitive athlete, and you are part of a total sum who make up only a small percentage of the total population. Let's assume that only 2 percent of people could be classified as such. Competitive athletes need lower body fat so that they can move faster. So, most competitive athletes will have a good weight, which is determined by the sport, how they train, and how they compete. For recreational athletes, a man's body weight should be between 10–20 percent fat, and a woman's should between 15–25 percent fat, depending on whether she is considered an ectomorph. A man's body fat percentage is a good guideline, even if they're not a recreational athlete. When people are not professional athletes, they will be considered as recreational athletes, which is based on just the normal day-to-day exercises at the gym. In fact, as I've been saying, the pursuit of fitness is something quite separate from athleticism.

So, let's look at body fat for the average population. There are many people who have more than 30 percent of body fat. In fact, 40 percent of body fat is considered obese. If you have more than 30 percent body fat, and you are distinctly overweight, it is unhealthy. It's going to reduce how long you live, and it's also going to cut down the quality of your life, every single day. It's far better to use body fat percentage as a guideline, without relying on the looks of your bone structure. If the percent of total body fat falls within an acceptable range, you will be considered to be at a healthy weight. If you're male, you have to be in the range of 10 to 15 percent body fat, and that is a good weight. If you are female, with less than 50 percent body fat, you'll tend to lose your menstrual cycle, which is not healthy. A proper body fat range would be between 10 to 30 percent, which is a pretty flexible range for all kinds of body types.

In reality, most people tend to fall in the 15–25 percent range. I would tell a man that if he reaches 20 percent body fat, he should start thinking about increasing exercise and decreasing his intake of calories now, before it gets out of control. I would also advise a woman that if she reaches 25 to 35 percent body fat, she needs to increase exercise and decrease her calorie intake. The variation of the 10-30 percent rule depends on different factors, like your gender, nutrition, background, age, and even your overall stress level. Once you drop below 10 percent body fat, you're underfed, which means that you are not getting enough nutrition. This condition only affects a very small percentage of the population, but the problem still remains that a majority of us are overfed.

Measurement techniques can tell you how much water is your body, and how much bone mass and muscle you have, to be a qualified competitor. Fitness professionals can help you determine your ratio of body fat, and your overall weight, through fitness methods. Knowing how much body fat you have is the starting point from where you begin to make healthy decisions. Taking action towards reducing excess fat is vital. You do not even have to take fat measurement tests; your mirror and clothes are a great sizing tool to let you know if you are gaining weight. If you look at your naked body in the mirror, and there's 2 or 3 inches of fat hanging over your waist line, it's likely that you have too much body fat.

The Best Is Yet to Come

When you visualize yourself, you take your life experiences into consideration, because that is a fraction of you. It's a way of factoring in what works in your life and what doesn't. It gives you a vision of the path on which your life is headed. It's like mapping out what you want for yourself on a vision board, and making sure that you are achieving those goals in a timely manner. It takes patience to achieve greatness. In order to achieve the best, you have to eliminate certain things that might prohibit you from getting you to achieve your best. In terms of fitness, when you have a goal of what you want your body to look like, you keep working hard to achieve that.

Having the mindset of "the more I exercise, the better I will look," will push you to achieve your best. It's a constant reminder for yourself to never quit, because the best is yet to come. Saying the phrase, "the best is yet to come," out loud, will be a motivation for you to continue on. The wonderful thought here is that some of the best days of our lives have not happened yet, and that's something to look forward to. While it might be easier to predict some of the same things we have experienced, you have to somehow believe that the best is coming, and that you are still learning and growing so that you can make better decisions, which will lead you to a better future.

André is a fun loving, authentic, creative, Jamaican man, who is passionate about health, wellness, and self-development. In his youth, he attended Knox Community College, in Mandeville, Manchester, Jamaica, while working in a dress making factory, using the experience he had gotten from his grandmother, who was a seamstress. At the age of 21, he started working in retail, and his boss decided to send the employees to the gym, to speed up production. André fell in love with fitness. It changed his perception of life. In 2007, he attended night school and obtained a diploma in Marketing and Sales. In 2008, he was promoted to retail buyer, which prepared him for Steele, his company today.

After about 10 years, he noticed that he looked as good as the models on the underwear boxes, and he decided to move to Canada to be an underwear model. In 2011, he arrived in Toronto, Ontario to follow his dream. He was told by modelling agencies that he was too short to be a model; however, he did become a fitness model, from 2012 to 2015. In 2013, André competed as a professional bodybuilder and won in the novice category. That same year, he read the book, *Think and Grow Rich*, by Napoleon Hill, and he decided he could become an underwear model by starting his own underwear company. As his thighs became more muscular, the crotch of his pants would wear out fairly quickly. He got curious about finding an underwear fabric that would help prevent this. He found that bamboo absorbs moisture, is sustainable, and is an eco-friendly fiber. The underwear, made with bamboo, helps the pants slide easier, and makes it more durable. All of André's underwear are made with bamboo for a comfortable, luxurious, and sexy feel.

Notes

Notes

Appendix "A" – Mind & Hydration

Hydration

- Water (When I feel hungry, I will first have a glass of water, then have a small meal)
- Lemon Water[1] (see Appendix "B" for recipe) (1 or 2 glasses first thing in the morning)
- Apple Cider Vinegar (ACV), with water (1 glass of water with 3 spoons of ACV before bed)
- Green drink – kale, apple, cucumber, carrot (2 days per week, I only drink a green liquid mix)
- Real homemade fruit drink, 3x per week (banana, strawberry, almond milk, honey, and ice or frozen fruit, blended)
- I consume a total of 6-8 glasses of water a day

Note: This helps keep me full and hydrated.

Eat

- Low carbs, always
- I only use honey to sweeten drinks or in food
- No more than 1 spoon of brown rice, maybe 3x max per week
- A half plate of salad with lunch and dinner
- A small portion of mostly chicken breast but other protein as well
- No more than 4 slices of bread per week
- I practice intermittent fasting; therefore, eating only between 11am–6pm

Note: I eat what I want in small portions, 4–5 times a day. I don't eat to get full but to feel satisfied.

How to Prevent Teeth Enamel Damage from lemon water

1. Dilute lemon juice in 8 oz of water – I would do 1/2 cup + 3 tbsp boiling water + rest cold water.
2. Drink lemon water with a straw.
3. Rinse your mouth with clear water right after drinking lemon water.
4. Avoid brushing teeth for 60 minutes after.
5. Use soft toothbrush and avoid aggressive brushing.

Mind

- I think slim
- I self-talk, and this helps me believe I am trimming up
- I look at positive body images every day, which motivates me to work for what I want
- I tell myself the truth: I know it will take about 3 weeks before I start feeling and noticing a difference
- I keep my eye on the prize, realizing my weight loss goal

Breathing exercises

- Deep breathing techniques are incredibly helpful.
- Try simple breathing exercises such as:
- Slowly inhaling while counting to 5 in your head.
- Hold your breath for 5 seconds then exhale slowly.
- Repeat this 10 times, whenever you feel your stress levels are going up.
- The breathing exercises may get you into a meditative state.

Appendix "B" – Recipes

Smoothie Drink Recipe (blender required)

Ingredients:

1 ripe banana
2 scoops of vanilla protein of your choice
Handful of a variety of salad topper, greens, baby carrots
1 teaspoon of fibre powder
2 teaspoons of honey or maple syrup (to taste)
Almond milk or unsweetened juice of your choice
1 tablespoon peanut butter
Handful of fresh or frozen fruit, ice as necessary
Vanilla and/or cinnamon to your taste

Instructions:

Peel banana, break into small chunks.
Add fruit, greens, carrots.
Add protein powder, flavorings to taste.
Add protein powder, peanut butter.
Top up with almond milk or juice.
Blend until silky smooth.
Enjoy.

Maple Citrus Salmon with Avocado-Orange Salsa

Ingredients [for salmon]:

4 salmon fillets
1/4 cup maple syrup
2 tablespoons orange juice
Sea salt and pepper
Cooking spray

Ingredients [For Avocado-Orange Salsa]:

2 large navel oranges peeled and diced into 1-inch cubes
2 avocados diced
2 tablespoons red onion diced
1/2 cup bell pepper diced
1 jalapeno seeded and diced
1 tablespoons lime juice
1/2 teaspoon salt

Instructions:

Preheat oven to 350°. Coat the bottom of a baking dish with cooking spray.
Lay salmon fillets in a single layer in the bottom of a baking dish, and season with sea salt and pepper.
In a bowl, whisk together maple syrup and juice. Pour over salmon fillets, allowing to rest for at least 10 minutes before baking.
Bake for 10-15 minutes, or until salmon flakes easily with a fork. [Internal temperature should be at least 145°]
Meanwhile, combine all ingredients for the salsa in a bowl and toss gently.
Remove salmon from the oven, plate and cover with a generous amount of the salsa.

Chili Mac - Makes two servings

Ingredients:

1 tablespoon olive oil
2 cloves garlic, minced
1 medium onion, diced
½ pound ounces lean ground beef
4 cups chicken or vegetable broth
1 500ml can diced tomatoes
¾ cup canned white kidney beans, drained
¾ cup canned kidney beans, drained
2 teaspoons chili powder
1 ½ teaspoon cumin
kosher salt and freshly ground black pepper, to taste
10 ounces elbows pasta
¾ cup shredded cheddar cheese
2 tablespoons chopped fresh parsley leaves

Instructions:

Heat olive oil in a large skillet or Dutch oven over medium-high heat. Add garlic, onion and ground beef, and cook until browned, about 3-5 minutes, making sure to crumble the beef as it cooks; drain excess fat.
Stir in broth, tomatoes, beans, chili powder and cumin; season with salt and pepper, to taste. Bring to a simmer and stir in pasta. Bring to a boil; cover, reduce heat and simmer until pasta is cooked through, 13-15 minutes.
Remove from heat. Top with cheese and cover until melted.
Serve immediately, garnish with parsley.

Green drink (blender required)

Ingredients:

Handful blueberries or other berries (frozen for a cool drink)
Handful kale, spinach or other greens
1 ripe banana
Half cup unsweetened almond milk
1 apple cored and sliced

Instructions:

Add all ingredients to blender.
Add some ice if desired.
Blend until silky smooth.

Real homemade fruit drink (blender required)

Ingredients:

One ripe banana
Handful strawberries or other fruit
250Ml almond milk
Cinnamon/vanilla to taste
A few ice cubes (or use frozen fruit)

Instructions:

Add all ingredients to blender.
Blend until silky smooth.
Add additional liquid if needed.

Lemon Water: *How to make lemon water at home.*

Ingredients:

1/2 lemon
1/4 cup cold water
1/3 cup boiling water

Instructions:

In a glass, squeeze lemon juice with lemon juice reamer or hand-held lemon reamer.
Discard seeds.
Add water, stir and drink while warm.

Remedies

Some common home remedies (note, for therapeutic use only) for some common ailments and for general health improvements. Blend or juice, consume immediately, refrigerate unused portions, use within 2-3 days.

Cold
- Carrot
- Pineapple
- Ginger
- Garlic
- Headache
- Apple
- Cucumber
- Kale
- Ginger
- Celery

Ulcers
- Cabbage
- Carrot
- Celery

High Blood Pressure
- Beet
- Apple
- Celery
- Cucumber
- Ginger
- Kidney Detox
- Carrot
- Watermelon
- Cucumber
- Cilantro

Eyes
- Carrot
- Celery

Constipation
- Carrot
- Apple
- Cabbage

Hangover
- Apple
- Carrot
- Beet
- Lemon

Nervousness
- Carrot
- Celery
- Pomegranate

Depression
- Carrot
- Apple
- Spinach
- Beet

Diabetes
- Carrot
- Spinach
- Celery

Asthma
- Carrot
- Spinach
- Apple
- Garlic

- Lemon
- Arthritis
- Carrot
- Celery
- Pineapple
- Lemon

Kidney Stones
- Orange
- Apple
- Watermelon
- Lemon

Stress
- Banana
- Strawberry
- Pear

Memory Loss
- Pomegranate
- Beets
- Grapes

Fatigue
- Carrots
- Beets
- Green Apple
- Lemon
- Spinach

Indigestion
- Pineapple
- Carrot
- Lemon
- Mint

Appendix "C" – Exercises & Stretches

Stretching Exercises

Side bends

The purpose of this exercise is to stretch the oblique muscles, as well as other muscles on the side of the torso.

Execution:
Stand upright, with feet slightly more than shoulder width apart.
raise your right arm over your head, and bend slowly to the left.
Letting your left hand slide down your thigh, bend as far as you can, and hold this position for about 35 seconds.
Return to stretching position and then repeat with the opposite side.

Forward bends

The purpose of this exercise is to stretch the hamstrings and lower back.

Execution:
Stand upright, with feet together.
Bend forward to take hold of the back of your legs, as far down as possible—knees, calves, or ankles—and pull gently with your arms, bringing in your arms as close as possible to your legs in order to stretch the lower back and hamstrings to their limit.
Hold this position for 35–65 seconds, and then relax.
Place one foot or ankle on a support.
Keeping your other leg straight, bend forward along the raised leg

and take hold of it as far down as possible—knee, calf, ankle, or foot—and pull gently to get the maximum stretch in the hamstring. Hold for about 35 seconds, relax, and then repeat the movement, using the other leg.

Lunges

The purpose of this exercise is to stretch the inner thighs, hamstrings, and glutes.

Execution:
Stand upright; move one leg forward, then bend that knee, coming down so that the knee of your trailing leg touches the floor.
Place your hand on either side of your front foot to get the maximum stretch of the inner thigh.
From this position, straighten your forward leg and lock your knee. Straighten the hamstring at the back of the leg.
Bring the other knee forward and lower yourself to the floor again. Repeat this movement, first straightening the leg, then coming down to the floor again.
Stand upright once more, step forward with the opposite, and repeat the stretching procedure.

Feet apart-seated forward bends

The purpose of this exercise is to stretch the hamstrings and lower back.

Execution:
Sit on the floor, with legs straight and wide apart.
Bend forward and touch the floor with your hands, as far in front of you as possible.
Hold this position for a few seconds, and then walk your hands over one leg.
Then grip it as far down as possible—knee, calf, or ankle—then pull

gently on your leg to get the maximum stretch of your hamstring and lower back.

Hold this position for about 35 seconds; then walk your hands over the other leg and repeat.

Inner thigh stretches

The purpose of this exercise is to stretch the inner thighs.

Execution:

Sit on the floor and draw your feet towards you, so the soles are touching.

Take hold of your feet; then pull them as close to the groin as possible.

Relax your legs and drop towards the floor, stretching the inner thighs.

Press down on your knees with your elbows to get a more complete stretch.

Hold for 35–65 seconds, and then relax.

Quadriceps stretches

The purpose of this exercise is to stretch the front of the thighs.

Execution:

Kneel on the floor and separate your feet enough so that you can sit between them.

Put your hands on the floor behind you and lean back as far as possible, feeling the stretch in the quadriceps.

Those who are less flexible will be able to lean back a little; those who are very flexible will be able to lay back on the floor.

Hold this position for 35–65 seconds, and then relax.

Spinal twist

The purpose of this exercise is to increase the rotational range of motion of the torso, and to stretch the outer thighs.

Execution:
Sit on the floor; with legs extended in front of you.
Bring your right knee up and twist around so that your left elbow rests on the outside of the upraised knee.
Place your right hand on the floor, and continue to twist to the right as far as possible.
Twist to the extreme of your range of motion and hold for 30 seconds.
Lower your right knee, bring up your left, and repeat the motion with the other side.

Seven Day Strength Training Plan
With minimal weights

Day 1

Phase 1	Phase 2	Phase 3	Phase 4	Phase 5
Cardio 5 Minutes	Standing Shoulder Press 5 Minutes	Squat 5 Minutes	Ab Crunch 5 Minutes	Cardio 5 Minutes
	The standing shoulder press with dumbbells exercise can be done unilaterally, meaning one arm at a time, or bilaterally, meaning both arms together. 1. The dumbbells start at shoulder level with your palms facing forward. 2. Press one arm or both dumbbells overhead, bringing the weights together until they almost touch overhead. 3. If you do the one-arm version, you can alternate arms or do all the repetitions for one arm and then switch sides.	1. Stand with dumbbell in each hand. 2. Bend Knees to a sitting position 3. Return to standing position 4. Repeat	1. Lie on your back with your feet against a wall (so your knees and hips are bent at a 90-degree angle) 2. Tighten your abdominal muscles and raise your head and shoulders off the floor 3. Try crossing your arms on your chest instead of behind your head (to avoid straining your neck) 4. Hold for about three deep breaths, lower to the ground, 5. repeat	

Day 2

Phase 1	Phase 2	Phase 3	Phase 4	Phase 5
Cardio 5 Minutes	Row 5 Minutes	Deadlift 5 Minutes	Side Bend 5 Minutes	Cardio 5 Minutes

Day 3

Phase 1	Phase 2	Phase 3	Phase 4	Phase 5
Cardio 5 Minutes	Bicep Curl 5 Minutes	Lying Tricep Extension 5 Minutes	Lower Body Crunch 5 Minutes	Cardio 5 Minutes

Day 4

Phase 1	Phase 2	Phase 3	Phase 4	Phase 5
Cardio	Shoulder Raise	Lunge	Ab Crunch	Cardio
5 Minutes	5 Minutes	5 Minutes (repeat other side)	Core Set Exercise	5 Minutes

Day 5

Phase 1	Phase 2	Phase 3	Phase 4	Phase 5
Cardio	Dumbbell Fly	Ribcage	Double Crunch	Cardio
5 Minutes	5 Minutes	5 Minutes	5 Minutes	5 Minutes

Day 6

Phase 1	Phase 2	Phase 3	Phase 4	Phase 5
Cardio	Dumbbell Fly	Ribcage	Double Crunch	Cardio
5 Minutes	5 Minutes	5 Minutes	5 Minutes	5 Minutes

Day 7

Phase 1	Phase 2	Phase 3	Phase 4	Phase 5
Cardio	Dumbbell Fly	Ribcage	Double Crunch	Cardio
5 Minutes	5 Minutes	5 Minutes	5 Minutes	5 Minutes

Exercises & Stretches

Workout Log Sheet

Visit	1		2		3		4		5		6		7		8		9		10		11		12	
Date																								
Cardio Warm Up																								
Fitness	Wt	Reps	Wt	Reps	Wt	Reps	Wt	Reps	Wt	Reps	Wt	Reps	Wt	Reps	Wt	Reps	Wt	Reps	Wt	Reps	Wt	Reps	Wt	Reps
Cardio Cool Down																								
Time Spent																								